¡Chistes!

¡Chistes!
HISPANIC HUMOR

of Northern New Mexico and Southern Colorado

Edited and Translated by

Nasario García

Foreword by

John Nichols

Museum of New Mexico Press   Santa Fe

To
Tom and Celia Chávez,
Two
Wonderful Friends

Contributors marked with an asterisk (*) are drawn from Juan B. Rael, *Cuentos españoles de Colorado y Nuevo México*, Vols. I & II, 2nd ed., © Museum of New Mexico Press.

Project editor: Mary Wachs
Design and production: Deborah Flynn Post
Manufactured in United States of America
10 9 8 7 6 5 4 3 2 1

Library of Congress Cataloging-in-Publication Data
Chistes! : Hispanic humor of northern New Mexico and southern Colorado / edited and translated by Nasario Garcia ; foreword by John Nichols.
  p. cm.
English and Spanish.
ISBN 0-89013-430-8 (clothbound ed. : alk. paper) — ISBN 0-89013-431-6 (paperbound ed. : alk. paper)
  1. Hispanic Americans—Folklore. 2. Hispanic Americans—Humor. 3. Oral tradition—New Mexico. 4. Oral tradition—Colorado. I. Garcia, Nasario.
GR111.H57C47 2004
398'.089'68789—DC22

                                        2004003367

Museum of New Mexico Press
Post Office Box 2087
Santa Fe, New Mexico 87504

Contents

▪ ▪ ▪ ▪ ▪ ▪ Contributors ▪ ▪ ▪ ▪ ▪

Page numbers refer respectively to English and Spanish entries.

*Contributors with an asterisk (*) are drawn from Juan B. Rael, *Cuentos Españoles de Colorado y Nuevo México*, Vols. 1 and 2, 2nd ed. (Santa Fe: Museum of New Mexico Press, 1977). The stories were collected either in 1930 or 1940, according to information provided under Acknowledgments in Volume I.

Foreword

When I moved to northern New Mexico thirty-three years ago, I immediately fell in with my neighbors and commenced laughing. Everybody had a sense of humor. The first time I cleaned an *acequia* (ditch) with thirty-five other guys including a passel of *viejitos* (old-timers), I heard enough raucous joking to fill a book like this twice over. I also listened to much hilarious and risqué *mitote* (gossip): It kept my ears blushing crimson for a year!

Since I was the only *gabacho* (Anglo) hefting a *pala* (shovel) that day, I took a lot of good-natured ribbing to boot. Though I spoke Spanish after a fashion, I must admit the punch lines kept zipping past my head like bullets fired from a high-powered deer rifle, and it was difficult for me to keep track.

What was *not* a stretch for me was entering the spirit of playfulness that defined my new friends and cohorts. I had landed in a community after my own heart, where folks understood how to deal with difficult times with great verve, a strong communal identification, and plenty of wacky (yet usually instructive) humor.

Everyone knew everybody else's business, and people wryly commented on that business nonstop, day and night. My *vecinos* (neighbors) handled various disasters with tears and guffaws; they met death with sadness and giggles; and the most devout parishioners around could also poke fun at the church, the priests, and each other. Each Félix, Melitón, and María was a storyteller and a historian, a poet and a prophet, and also a stand-up comedian.

One old acquaintance of mine walked across a bridge over the Pueblo River to sing humorous *corridos* (ballads) in my driveway. Another ancient pal was a genius at writing biting political fables. My elderly friend Andrés Martínez used to make light whenever La Sebastiana (death) harvested another of his octogenarian buddies, saying, "Hey, I ducked so she missed me with her sickle and got Don Abenicio instead!"

When spring floods annually washed out the *compuerta* (sluice) on our acequia, the old *mayordomo* (ditch foreman or boss) and the rest of us, cursing and hee-hawing like drunken sailors, would thrash around in the icy river water trying to repair the damage, while mockingly berating ourselves for being inept stooges who could never seem to permanently solve the situation.

Wakes especially were a time of noisy grieving and also imaginative tale-telling: I'm surprised nobody ever put earmuffs on the nearby cadavers to protect their sensibilities from our irreverence.

Cows, horses, pigs, and other animals were always getting in trouble also, which was easy pickin's for the local pundits and punsters. "I live in Peñasco," one amigo regularly told me, "where the men are men and the sheep are really scared."

Most of the old-timers who welcomed me so warmly and humorously to New Mexico are gone now, but their spirits live on. And this wonderful book of *chistes* (jokes) has a bit of everything in it that still makes up the history and culture and humor of the place where I live. Some of the jokes remind me of the Little Moron or Little Audrey tales from my goofy, misspent childhood. Others will leave you delightfully puzzled and mystified, as after a baffling shaggy-dog story. Often the humor is gentle, touching on emotional chords that travel deep and have been strong for centuries. Then again, from time to time there is childish delight in innocent smut for the sake of innocent smut, similar to kids having a farting contest after lights-out at summer camp.

Naturally, God gets in His (or Her) licks and is also soundly punted around on occasion. Tottering geezers play the dozens with each other. *Políticos* take it in *la oreja* (ear). Eggs, called *huevos*, are often delightfully confused with testicles, which are also called huevos. Don Cacahuate and Doña Cebolla—Mr. Peanut and Mrs. Onion—are often called forth acting like idiots, usually while stumbling down a railroad track about to get broadsided by a huge locomotive.

There's a lot of kidding around with *santos* (images of saints), plenty of coy comments on infidelity, a kid who wants to marry his grandmother, a gay rooster, a lawyer, a doctor, and a shepherd locked in a room with a skunk. Too, burros make plenty of appearances . . . cowboys take a bit of guff . . . a guy marooned in the desert is bitten by a snake . . . and a cellular telephone falls into a bedpan filled with urine! A funny play on words earns two destitute musicians a job on a big-city trolley car.

For good measure, Don Cacahuate pays a return visit trying to pilot his motorcycle at night between the headlights of two approaching motorbikes. Unfortunately, those approaching headlights actually belong to a single automobile! One of my favorite stories concerns a tin can full of dung and a little black cricket hanging from the king's castle's *vigas* (wooden beams).

As you can see, the laughter never stops. The Spanish versions of these tales are particularly funny, pungent, and interesting because they are recounted in colorful local vernaculars that are heard nowhere else on earth.

Much that identifies and reinforces indigenous culture lies beneath this monkey business. Sometimes the stories are fey personal reminiscences that make you smile and also break your heart a little bit. Overall, this book is a precious gift that captures the comic and mischievous soul of a people and, ultimately, the serious soul as well. By the end of all the uproarious *cuentitos* (anecdotes), you will hope fervently that these irreverent men and women, their culture, and their *patria chica* (hometown or area) will go on forever, giving balance and love and much laughter to us all.

John Nichols
Taos, New Mexico

Acknowledgments

I should like to pay special tribute to those old-timers (*viejitos*) who have passed on to a better life since speaking with them. They have left us and future generations oral accounts replete with laughter and joy.

Other *viejitos* whom I also had the distinct pleasure of interviewing during the past thirty years who appear in this book also deserve to be recognized for their generous repertoire of anecdotes. The enjoyment they derived from seeing me laugh at their witticisms brought not just a twinkle to their eyes but a sense of gratification as well. Even the most serious and dignified informants, when asked about a joke or two or something funny, suddenly assumed a comical disposition and transformed themselves into waggish sorts of characters. It was wonderful to witness this kind of change as they showed off their own brand of humor.

A particular person who also merits special mention among my interviewees is Juanita Malouff-Domínguez from Chama, Colorado, in the San Luis Valley. She credits her mother, Susana Gonzales-Malouff, and her grandmother, Isidora Romero-Gonzales (Mama Lola), for having shared with her the wonderful stories that appear in my book.

Two individuals who warrant being singled out for their kind help in this project are Alana Palomino and Joanna Vidaurre-Trujillo. The lovely and lively humorous stories that people in Alana's community of Ratón, New Mexico, shared with me are due solely to her efforts. As for Joanna, from Llano de San Juan Nepomuceno, I offer my heartfelt thanks for bringing her mother's stories to my attention.

Lastly, I wish to express my sincere gratitude to Anna Gallegos, Director, Museum of New Mexico Press, and to Mary Wachs, Editorial Director, two glowing lights throughout the process of seeing *!Chistes!* evolve from start to finish. I would also like to thank designer Deborah Flynn Post and marketing director Daniel Kosharek for lending a helping hand in my project.

■ ■ ■ ■ Introduction ■ ■ ■ ■

Humor has been part of Hispanic culture—from Spain and Latin America to the American Southwest—from time immemorial. From creative literature, folk culture, and the entertainment world to the individual in the street, humor abounds and comprises a vital part of the Hispanic psyche. Even today, Don Quixote, Sancho Panza, and Cantinflas (Mario Moreno Reyes) continue to be shining examples of humor, and they are household names throughout the Spanish-speaking world, including the southwestern United States. In the seventeenth century, Sancho Panza had a seemingly inexhaustible repertoire of humorous folk sayings in counseling Don Quixote, the knight errant, who was himself a purveyor—and victim—of humor, while Cantinflas, the twentieth-century Mexican film star, immortalized the *pelado* (penniless) in his classic comic routines.

¡Chistes!: Hispanic Humor of Northern New Mexico and Southern Colorado brings together for the first time in Spanish and English a medley of voices of laughter and comic relief from these two geographical regions, where Hispanic culture is struggling to maintain its identity. One must recognize that this collection is minuscule compared to the huge range of humor in the rest of the Hispanic world, but nevertheless, *¡Chistes!* does provide an important sampling of Hispanic humor in general and throughout northern New Mexico and southern Colorado in particular.

Humor in the Hispanic villages of these two culturally rich areas goes back a long time. Through good and difficult times, Hispanos have always been able to laugh, not only with each other and those around them but at themselves as well. In addition to jokes and humorous tales, humor can also be found in various facets of folklore such as folk sayings (*dichos*), riddles (*adivinanzas*), and love quatrains (*chiquiaos*).

The *Diccionario de la Real Academia Española* (*DRAE*) (*Dictionary of the Spanish Royal Academy*) defines *chiste* as an "*historieta muy breve que contiene un juego verbal o conceptual capaz de mover a risa"* ("a brief anecdote that contains a verbal or conceptual game capable of engendering laughter"). This book, therefore, is not limited strictly to jokes per se. For our purpose, the word *chiste* is used with the broad definition provided by the Spanish Royal Academy; hence, it serves both as a convenient title and as a framework for a variety of comical events that are typical among Hispanics of northern New Mexico and southern Colorado.

Approximately one-third of the contributors to this collection come from southern Colorado. Collectively, all the interviewees offer us a potpourri of funny experiences, some real, others imagined or part of folklore tradition. Humor comes in different forms, and the chistes range from practical jokes, pranks, slip-of-the-tongue jokes, hyperbole, solecisms (i.e., grammatical blunders or language misunderstandings), slapstick humor, and double entendre to self-denigration and malapropisms.

The tone of each story varies accordingly. At times the humor may be gentle, kind, or blatant, while other times it is witty or even wistful. Biting and harsh humor, as seen in Virginia Alfonso's dialogue story *"Sarcasmo de una pareja,"* as well as irony, mimicry, and wit, can be found in the tales that follow. The person(s) at the center of attention may differ from one story to another, but the medium of humor, overt or subtle, remains constant throughout the book.

Not all the stories in *¡Chistes!* are suitable for every age group, but there are funny tales for everyone to enjoy—from small children and adolescents to grown-ups. Although some stories are simple and innocent enough to read to small children, the majority is more fitting for young and older adults.

Much Hispanic humor in both states stems from everyday life or local folk culture. Occasionally, though, a story from Spain, such as Eduardo Valdez's *"Dos jóvenes que querían ser astrónomos"*/"Two Aspiring Young Astronomers," shows up in a remote village like Ojo del Padre in the Río Puerco Valley. In many ways the humor reflected in this collection is reminiscent of the eighteenth-century Spanish dramatist Ramón de la Cruz (1731–1794). By utilizing different *tipos* (types)—for example, street vendors and barbers—in his *sainetes* (one-act plays in which the comic element prevails), he was able to poke fun at social vices and abuses. In ¡Chistes!, the shepherd, the deaf person (political correctness was not in vogue in previous generations), the priest, the politician, and the pícaro (rogue), among others, are subject to ridicule in amusing and entertaining ways, and therefore they can be seen among Hispanics as types of characters in everyday life or as part of folklore.

The local church and its priest, central to the life of an Hispanic village, have never been immune from social criticism, a phenomenon that takes us back to Spanish medieval literature, for example, the Arcipreste de Hita's El libro de buen amor. Priests in particular, although the most venerated and respected members of a local Hispanic community, were nevertheless exposed to mockery in more than one good-natured way. ¡Chistes! contains several humorous encounters about or with priests, some of which poke fun at their questionable behavior, as in the story "Entró al confesonario"/ "He Entered the Confessional" by Andrés Archuleta. In this story the priest unwittingly switches places with the confessor, only to find himself in an untenable and embarrassing position because of his own personal transgressions.

In some narratives the emphasis shifts from the priest to the local santos (sacred images of saints), but he still remains a central figure. Sometimes introducing the santos merely illustrates how sacred images can be used in a nonsacrilegious way to evoke laughter among the local people. After all, "punishing" santos (by facing them to the wall or hiding them in a footlocker) for not answering supplications (e.g., rain for crops) was not unusual, and thus using them to conjure up laughter was fair game as well.

It should be noted that some stories here involve animals versus humans. At times the animal is ridiculed, appearing to be the victim of circumstances; while other times it is the man (hardly ever a woman) who comes across as a veritable buffoon and a casualty of his own intellectual shortcomings or ineptitude.

A fair share of jokes also centers on the play on words, that is, the use or misunderstanding of language. Many punch lines or endings to a comical event hinge on a variety of linguistic nuances. A play on words, as in the imperative form *escoja* (select) and *es coja* (she is lame), is a good illustration of gentle or wry humor. Slips of the tongue such as *"Padre Nuestro/Pedo Nuestro* (Our Father/Fart Father)" are not common or surprising either, but funny given the Hispano penchant for levity.

Double entendre is also an inducement to laughter. For example, in the story *"El Cholesterol"* by Filiberto Esquibel, the onus clearly is on the word *huevos* (eggs), whose intended meaning—and the punch line to the tale—is shrouded in the sexual connotation of *huevo*, meaning ball, a euphemism for testicle. It should be pointed out that not all instances of double meaning focus on the risqué or indecorous. In fact, only a handful of narratives scattered throughout *¡Chistes!* could be considered outright scatological. As one woman told me, *"Tengo munchos chistes, pero los murre feos se quedan en casa conmigo"* ("I have lots of jokes, but the real nasty ones stay at home with me").

But language conflict or miscommunication is not restricted only to Hispanics. These phenomena transcend Spanish speakers per se and occasionally include the three principal groups living in New Mexico: Anglos, Hispanics, and Indians. An Hispano whose knowledge of English is minimal or nonexistent is just as likely to be the brunt of a joke as an Anglo who knows little or no Spanish. At the very least, encounters involving Hispanics and Anglos could be categorized as cross-cultural, bilingual or bicultural, or both. Felipe Cantú's *"El mejicano que creía que sabía hablar inglés"*/"The Mexican Who Thought He Knew English," and *"Las sardinas"*/"The Sardines" by Lucinda Atencio, are but two hilarious examples of laughter across cultures. These types of jokes should surprise no one familiar with New Mexican culture. Most of them are told in jest and are devoid of any derogatory racial implications.

More modern American influences affecting Hispanic culture can be seen in other, if limited ways. *"Dos Hippies"* and *"El telefón celular"* by Elba C. de Baca and Fred W. Korte, respectively, are prime examples. These stories not only amuse because of their humor, but they are timely due to their subject matter, which ostensibly falls outside Hispanic tradition but nevertheless reflects modern-day realities in American society that affect Hispanos.

The Hispano's ability to laugh at himself is demonstrated in episodes involving disputes between husband and wife, in which the woman tacitly or openly plays the central figure. Male chauvinism, a cultural attribute among Hispanic males that is often used as a façade to keep their egos publicly intact—at a woman's expense—is vividly portrayed in quick-witted fashion in José Nataleo Montoya's story *"¡Que se vaya al infierno!"* / "She Can Go to Hell!" On other occasions a husband's self-avowed virility is pared down to size by his wife, who is fed up with his drunken sprees and shenanigans, as we see in Alicia Romero-Vidaurre's comical *"En un tanto cuanto"* / "In a Jiffy." In Lucinda Atencio's *"El zancarrón"* / "The Lean Bone," the adulterous wife ironically emerges as more quick-witted and hence the victor in the midst of an extramarital crisis.

These brief comments on the spirit of Hispanic humor and how it functions provide only a quick glance at the diversity of stories found in *¡Chistes!: Hispanic Humor of Northern New Mexico and Southern Colorado.* The examples given serve as snapshots at best to highlight certain types of humor, but they hardly encapsulate the scope of the stories Hispanic old-timers have shared with me.

Unlike longer, more protracted narratives in which the raconteurs spin and weave more sophisticated plots, in *¡Chistes!*, because of the nature of the genre, the joke teller usually just goes to the heart of the story, then proceeds to the climax (i.e., the punch line). The development is simple and unobtrusive and not always replete with details or embellishment. The narrators, while hardly professional storytellers (or in this case joke tellers), possess a certain deftness for relaying their humorous stories in a precise, methodical fashion that is pleasing to the reader. Perhaps these are qualities inherent in old-timers with a gift, or *don,* for telling jokes. In fact, there seems to be at the very least a hint of underlying rascality in each one of them, regardless of gender.

As I reflect on the dozens of old-timers I have interviewed over the past several decades, those with humorous stories stand out if for no other reason than due to their outgoing personalities. Furthermore, they seem to look at life through a different set of philosophical lenses, without taking themselves too seriously. They have learned that being able to find humor even in adverse circumstances is the most propitious help in getting through life's trials. Their tales teach us, among other things, that a humorless existence on this earth is humdrum and, at worst, rueful. The jokes in *¡Chistes!* simply turn tedium on its head.

With the exception of a few contributors whose accounts come from Juan B. Rael's *Cuentos españoles de Colorado y Nuevo México (Spanish Folk Tales from Colorado and New Mexico*, published by Museum of New Mexico Press, second edition, 1997), and Philomeno Sánchez's *Don Phil-O-Meno sí la mancha* (San Luis, Colo.: Sangre de Cristo Printing, 1977), the rest come from my own oral history interviews conducted between 1978 and 2002. A handful of comical tales have appeared in previous, now out-of-print publications of mine, but the majority of those offered here are new and hitherto unpublished.

As a consequence, the preponderance of interviewees is also new to the reading public. They consist of men and women from different geographic areas of northern New Mexico and southern Colorado whose ages ranged from the sixties to the nineties. Some are still living, but others have passed on since the interviews were conducted. Virtually all of them hail from hamlets unfamiliar to most of us; some no longer dot the map. Most of the old-timers abandoned their birthplaces long ago and moved to larger cities or towns such as Albuquerque, Bernalillo, Las Vegas, New Mexico, Denver, or Pueblo, Colorado. Notwithstanding their relocation, they, like their compatriots who continue living in small communities, still cling faithfully, if precariously, to their customs, religion, and language.

The Spanish they speak by all measurements is quite standard and could be understood anywhere in the Spanish-speaking world. On the other hand, it is also special since their lexicon still contains an assortment of archaisms that date back centuries, as well as countless folk sayings and idiomatic expressions traceable to Spain, although many were born in New Mexico and Colorado. Mexicanisms and Anglicisms, coupled with the New Mexican Indian influence, also bring us closer to home.

The format offered in *¡Chistes!* is straightforward. Contributors are listed in alphabetical order, followed by their place of birth (some preferred to have both their birthplace and current place of residence listed). Their stories, if more than one, are in random order and presented in English translation in the first part of the book, followed by the Spanish version in the second half. This dichotomous approach helps maintain continuity from narrator to narrator and story to story and consequently lessens distractions by reading the stories in one language at a time. Furthermore, the purpose for presenting the narratives in both languages is twofold: to reach out to a readership that is literate in Spanish and to invite the monolingual English speaker—both Hispanic and non-Hispanic—to enjoy a bit of Hispanic culture along with a chuckle or two.

A challenging aspect in transcribing the taped interviews, all conducted in Spanish, invariably was to maintain the integrity of the language and, by extension, the content of the interviews without compromising the contributor's spoken words. With regard to the stories here, the task was facilitated because of their brevity and simple structure. The shorter the story, the less susceptible the narrator was to repeating pause words (e.g., *pues*, *pus*, or *pos*), thereby minimizing linguistic distractions that might impede the natural flow of a story.

Translating the stories from Spanish to English was also less troublesome because of their length, although admittedly the high point or punch line can be lost because of linguistic nuances that cannot be translated into English. To remedy this dilemma, an explanation is rendered in parentheses. Hopefully this will help keep the humor somewhat intact in the English translation, but in several stories the reader may have to use his or her imagination to appreciate the witticism.

Because of its idiosyncratic nature, the Spanish dialect of northern New Mexico and southern Colorado merits special attention, and for this reason I have added a glossary that juxtaposes standard or modern Spanish with the regional dialect. A linguist or reader competent in Spanish will thus be able to readily discern the difference between regional and local dialectology vis-à-vis more universal usage. Doing so makes reading *¡Chistes!* in Spanish much more pleasurable.

The voices that echo all through this volume are those of our old-timers—our *viejitos*. Their laughter sings to us and tickles our funny bones, for their giggling and chuckling came from jubilant hearts and souls. To listen to each of them share their stories was truly wonderful, for they brought smiles not only to their own faces but to mine and the family members present as well. After all is said and done, there is no substitute for the old-timers. Although their voices one day will be silent, we can take comfort in knowing that their words of joy and amusement are hereby recorded for us and for future generations to enjoy.

¡ Chistes !

Hispanic humor

Manuel B. Alcón
Ocaté/Mora, NM

■ A Precocious Little Boy

This little boy was always asking questions because he wanted answers. He sometimes went to visit his aunt María, who wasn't very fond of cleaning house. One day he went to visit her, and when he came back from his outing he asked his mother if it was true that we came from dirt or dust.

His mother told him yes. Then he asked her if we're going to turn to dust, and his mother responded yes.

"Dust we are, and dust is what we shall return to."

"Well, did you know that there's someone underneath my aunt María's bed?"

"Really?" said his mother.

"And not only that, the person who comes and goes must be very large," said the little boy.

"What makes you say that?" asked the mother.

"Because of the large pile of dirt under my aunt María's bed!"

■ The Know-It-All Scientists

These two educated professors, after having tossed God out from the schools and public offices, decided that they could now compete with God. They confronted Saint Peter at the Pearly Gates.

"What brings you here?" asked Saint Peter.

"We want to speak with God," said one of them.

"Wait just a moment," responded Saint Peter.

Then he got on the Internet and sent God an e-mail. God responded right away, and He said to them, knowing that the two professors were in cahoots:

"What's your problem? You already know that you're not on very good speaking terms with me."

"Well, we came to tell you that we no longer need You," said one of the scientists. "We already know how to do everything that needs to be done and possibly better than You. We've already been to the moon, we've invented atomic power, and now we've cloned many animals and people."

"Very well," said God. "But your word alone doesn't satisfy me in the least. Let's see if you can offer me some proof."

"What proof do you need?" said one of them.

"For you to build me a man made of dirt," said God.

"Kids' stuff!" said the more knowledgeable of the scientists.

They went outside and God said to them:

"Let's see what you can do!"

One of them started to make a pile of dirt. Then God said to them:

"Stop right there! This is my dirt. You invent your own."

■ A Frog

All of the little creatures from the forest got together and had a class. In came the professor, who was a lion, and said to them:

"Today we're going to entertain ourselves in the river. There's going to be lots of jokes."

"Oh, that's great!" said the frog. "How beautiful!"

"And afterwards we're going to the store and I'm going to treat you," said the lion.

"Oh, that's great!" said the frog.

And so it went. Every time the professor said something, the frog would say, "Oh, that's great!"

Finally the lion professor got tired of promising them all kinds of stuff and he said:

"As for that big mouth, we're not going to take him."

Then the frog said:

"Boy, the crocodile really got screwed!"

■ Three Persons

There were these three persons walking down the railroad tracks. One was a New Mexican, another one was a Californian, and the third one was a Texan. There they were walking when suddenly it got dark, really dark. The weather was a little bad. It looked like it was going to rain. They continued walking and came upon a ranch. They knocked at the door and out came a rancher who said to them:

"What's going on?"

"We have walked all day," said one of them. "We're very tired and we don't have a place to stay. So if you could put us up for the night . . . "

So the little old man, the rancher, said to them:

"Of course. The only thing is that I don't have but one bed, and only two of you fit in it. But I have a pigsty. I have a small pig. If you wish to spend the night with us here, you're welcome." And the three said in unison:

"Yes, something is better than nothing."

"Okay," said the rancher. "You can take turns. While one of you goes to the pigsty, the other two can sleep in the small sofa—the bed."

Very well. The three of them agreed on the swap, and the New Mexican got to go first. He went to the pigsty. Two minutes later he was back and he said:

"No way. I can't stand that pig anymore. Now it's your turn."

The Californian went next. He went in and joined the little pig. Three or four minutes later, he was back. Then it was the Texan's turn. He went in where the little pig was. There he was. The other two looked at the clock three minutes later. All of a sudden they heard banging at the door. It sounded like someone was trying to knock it down. They opened the door and in came the little pig with his nose covered, and he said:

"I don't know about you, but if that Texan were a pig, even we couldn't stand him!"

A Shark

There were these three friends on a small boat: a Mexican, an Italian, and a Frenchman. There they were floating when the boat began to sink. The small boat went under, so they started to swim. Then a shark came upon them, caught the Mexican, and ate him up. Then it caught the Italian. The shark ate him as well, but he let the Frenchman go. Then one of the other sharks said to the shark:

"Why didn't you eat the Frenchman?"

"No way," he said. "Why, my rear end still hurts from the last Frenchman I ate."

This Spoiled Little Brat

There was this spoiled little brat throwing a temper tantrum. I believe he was even saying bad words. The priest stopped by, and the little boy said to him:

"Listen, Father! Do you tell lies?"

And the father says to him:

"No. I'm not allowed to tell lies."

"And by the way, do you know lots about religion?"

"Yes, yes, why of course. I'm a priest. That was my calling."

"Well, where is God?"

"God is everywhere."

"And is He at my home?"

"Yes, yes, He's at your home."

"And on the road?"

"Yes, He's on the road."

"In my uncle's corral?"

"Yes, He's also in your uncle's corral."

"There, you see, you do lie," said the little boy. "Why, my uncle doesn't even have a corral!"

■ An Indian

This Indian wanted to become a Christian and he was taken to catechism. He was indoctrinated. By the time the priests thought he was ready for his first Holy Communion, one of the priests took him before the archbishop. The archbishop asked him to recite the prayers, and he knew them very well. Then he says to him:

"Do you know the creed?" and the Indian said yes, and he recited it to the archbishop.

"Do you believe in God?"

"Yes, yes, I do."

"And do you believe that God will judge the living and the dead?"

"Why, of course I do," he said to him. "But you mark my word, He won't show up!"

■ Wearing a Loincloth

This joke is about an Indian who was wearing a loincloth. This Mexican came up to him and said:

"Listen here, Indian, why is it that you don't wear clothes? There you are showing your bare ass. Aren't you cold?"

And the Indian says to him:

"No. My buttock like your face!"

Virginia Alfonso
Pueblo, CO

■ A Couple's Sarcasm

Husband:	Where's my deodorant so that I can smell nice and please the girls?
Wife:	Which one, dear? The roll-on?
Husband:	No, the one for the armpits.
Wife:	You didn't even say good morning.
Husband:	Well, good morning.
Wife:	Good-day greetings belong to God and not to the devil. As soon as you say good morning, you add politely, "May God grant you a good day."
Husband:	Agreed. I'll start all over again. May God grant you a good day. How are you this morning?
Wife:	Lying down. Do you think I sleep standing up?
Husband:	What's wrong with you? You talk as though you ate dog meat.
Wife:	Why, my dear? Are you missing a piece?
Husband:	Do you know something? You have your own ways just like you have your own face.
Wife:	Oh, you and your protruding nose! I've been meaning to ask you if that's your own or if it's a banana you're eating?
Husband:	Oh, kiss my whatchamacallit.
Wife:	Darling, I would do it, but have you forgotten that it's part of what you're missing? It's what they took out to mend your face.
Husband:	A barking dog doesn't bite.
Wife:	Go to hell!

Husband:	That's where I came from, but you weren't there.
Wife:	My father was right. I should never have gotten married.
Husband:	Mine was right also. He advised me that when choosing a puppy, to make sure the bitch was not a runt.
Wife:	Well, what happened? Why didn't he follow his own advice?
Husband:	I'll never beg you, even if I'm overcome with lice and even die of sadness.
Wife:	Well, start getting ready to die all infested.
Husband:	Who would have thought that this is how I'd end up? And to think of how much I used to like your kisses!
Wife:	Yes, but since you shaved off your mustache, your kisses are like an egg without salt.
Husband:	Damn woman! When I first met you, you seemed so meek.
Wife:	Donkeys are donkeys (i.e., idiots are idiots) but if you pester them long enough they finally kick you.
Husband:	Have you had enough?
Wife:	If you keep on with those insults, you're going to lose me.
Husband:	Much more was lost in the flood (Day of Judgment), and nothing belonged to me.
Wife:	That's it! Let's cut out the nonsense. We got married, and that's that. What would you like for breakfast? The sky's the limit!

Jesusita Aragón
Las Vegas, NM

■ Eleven Goats

One time a teacher asked a boy, who seemed a bit slow,

"If there were a herd of eleven goats in a corral and one took off, how many goats would be left?"

And the boy said:

"Not a one!"

The reason being, the other goats always follow the leader. That's goats for you!

■ A Sand Hill

This man was a professor at a college, and there were lots of students. Among them was this poor soul and nobody paid attention to him, as is usually the case. There's always one just like him. This boy was very quiet. The professor then said to himself: "I'm going to find out just how much these students know." And he said to them:

"Boy and girls. Listen. I'm going to ask you a question. Way off in the distance there's a sand hill. How many sacks will it take to use up the sand from that sand hill?"

Some said ten, others said one hundred, and so on. Then the professor said to himself, "I'm going to go ask that one, the quiet one," and he did.

"And what have you got to say for yourself? What do you think? How many sacks will it take to use up the sand from that sand hill?"

And the quiet one says:

"Well, I'll tell you what. If the sack is as large as the sand hill, all you need is one."

My Compadre Jesús

One time my compadre Jesús' sisters-in-law went to visit him. He was at a hospital over in Colorado. That's where he and his wife lived. The sisters-in-law went to pay him a visit, and he was wearing one of those hospital gowns, and so one of them said to him:

"Señora Santana,
Señor San José,
lower your leg,
for I can see
all of your peg."

And he said to her:

"Señora Santana,
Señor San José,
stop staring,
it's not for you anyway,
so it matters not
if it's seen."

A Cornhusk

What I'm about to tell you happened right here in Las Vegas. This man was a very good friend of a judge whose name was Don Luis Armijo. And Don Luis was very mean-spirited, but he was a good friend of this man's relatives, and the poor man, a rancher, didn't know what to answer in court. I don't know why he had to appear in court.

"Come here, Segundo," Segundo Baca, was his name. "Look, if a rancher uses cornhusks to roll a cigarette, how many licks does he need to seal the cigarette?"

"Listen, Don Luis, my friend. If he drools as much as you, all he needs is one good lick. One good lick will do."

Johnnie Archibeque
Bernalillo, NM

■ The Cows

This woman and some other women worked for the priest. One day he asked each family to donate an animal, at least one cow. When the woman got home, she told her husband that he has to donate the cow, which was the only milk cow they had. The husband refused, but the wife begged him so much that he finally gave in to her. Well, as it turned out, she gathered quite a herd for the priest.

Then the husband talked to a cowherd about taking care of the cows. One summer day the cowherd fell asleep under a tree, and all the cows took off for the corral since they knew their way back. The cows had been gone for quite a while. They all followed the husband's cow and headed for the corral where the cow was before being given away.

The wife had told the husband that God was going to reward them if they donated their cow. One morning the husband was shaving and saw that the corral was full of cattle. He then said to his wife:

"You were right when you said that God was going to reward us. Look at all the cows in the corral!"

When the cowherd found out that they were in the corral, he went after them. The husband refused to give them back. He says to the cowherd:

"You mean to tell me the priest is lying! He told us that God was going to reward us, and those are the cows He gave me."

The priest, wanting to settle the matter, then said:

"The one who greets me good morning first tomorrow morning gets to keep the cows."

As it happened, near the portal to the priest's house there was a very leafy tree. That night the husband went and hid himself in the tree. In the morning when the priest went outside, the husband jumped down from the tree and caught the priest by surprise:

"Good morning, Father!" and so he got to keep all the cows.

■ The Table Is a Companion

The table is always a companion to the chair. One day the chair was mad at the table, and so the table asked the chair what was wrong:

"Why are you mad at me?"

The chair answered:

"At least the cook sets a plate on you, but as for me, all she does is plop her butt on me!"

■ My Dog Has a Fever

The boyfriend invited his girlfriend to the movies and to dinner, and when he went to pick her up at her house, she says to him:

"Honey, I can't go with you because my dog has a fever, and I'll have to take him to the doctor."

The boyfriend says to her:

"You don't have to go to all that expense. Just go to the refrigerator and grab the mustard."

"And why the mustard?" says the girlfriend.

"That's what you put on a hotdog!"

Andrés Archuleta
Trujillo, NM

■ Two Old Men Basking in the Sun

Okay, I'm going to tell you something silly. There were these two old men basking in the sun, because they weren't worth a hoot for anything anymore. They were chatting, you know? And two old ladies went by and saw the old men, and they said to themselves:

"Let's make these old fellows look up."

Well, the old men were already quite old, like me. And so the old ladies went and got all dolled up. They got all dressed up, they put on their hats and all, and so they went by where the old men were. One of them lifted his head and said:

"Look!" he said to the other old man. "My, but aren't they all dressed up."

But that was it! And so the old ladies said:

"Now, what do you think of that? They didn't even get up or anything."

Next day the old ladies commented:

"Well, let's see if we can get them to get up."

They went and put on these, what I call, "picnicks." What are they called? Shorts. And there they were, the old men, like always, doing nothing. The old ladies went by one more time, and one of the old men saw them.

"Look at that!" he said to his fellow companion. "Why, they didn't even iron their clothes!"

You see, the legs were nothing but wrinkles.

■ The Flour Tortilla

This story is about Don Cacahuate and Doña Cebolla. They both had a little boy, and he was crying a lot because he wanted a tortilla, you see? So Don Cacahuate said to Doña Cebolla:

"What's wrong with this boy that he doesn't stop crying?"

She said to him:

"He's crying because you gave him a cold tortilla."

"Oh, shit!" he responded.

He grabbed the tortilla and stuck it under his armpit. Then he said to the child:

"Here, take it!"

The child took it.

"Now what's wrong?" said the father.

"I burnt myself."

■ He Entered the Confessional

There were these neighbors, and one of them claimed, he was almost sure, that his neighbor had stolen his cow and he didn't quite know how to get the truth out of him. Then the one with the stolen cow went to the father, the local priest, and said to him:

"Father, I'm almost sure that that neighbor of mine stole my cow. Why don't you confess him? Hear his confession to see if you can get the truth out of him."

Well, soon thereafter everyone started to work on him—the same one who had stolen the cow—egging him on. He wasn't used to going to confession, but the people kept after him:

"You better go to confession, you better . . . "

Finally they convinced him, and he went to confession. He went inside the confessional, and the priest said to him:

"Well, your neighbor says that you stole his cow."

The man didn't respond. It was about that time that a new confessional had been installed in the church. And the priest said to him once more:

"Word's going around that you stole the peasant's cow."

He didn't answer. Then the priest came out from inside the confessional and said to him:

"Listen. I'm talking to you. Can't you hear?"

"No," said the man. "I can't hear. It's hard to hear."

"What do you mean you can't hear?"

"No, I can't," he said to the priest. "You get in there! Then I'll hear you confess," said the peasant.

So the priest exchanged places with him. Then the man with the cow said to him:

"People are all saying that you're living with the mother superior."

The priest didn't answer. And the man repeated once again:

"People are saying that you're sleeping with the mother superior."

The priest didn't answer. Then the man came around and said to him:

"Didn't you hear?"

"No," said the priest. "This confessional isn't working. I'm going to request that they install another one."

Miguel Antonio Arellano
Amalia, NM/Pueblo, CO

■ **Here's Your Tacho!**

Once upon a time, a long time ago, there were these people, Indians, who lived in Farmington. They used to plant a little bit at a time. The Indians planted corn, and their crop supposedly was quite good. Well, there was this Indian who planted his corn and the ears of corn came out very quickly. The yield was so good that when the Anglos went by they started to steal ears of corn from him. They had gotten into the habit of stealing his corn.

This Anglo woman then went to steal corn, and so this Indian went to the cornfield and was already waiting for her. Here she was gathering corn while the Indian took off his clothes, piece by piece. By the time she already had her arms full of corn to take with her, he took off after her naked as a jaybird. She was running away from him. Back then people were all Catholic. She was fleeing and the Indian was about to catch her, and she blurted out:

"Holy Father of San Acacio, free me from this Indian!"

"Here's your Tacho!" he responded. "This is your Tacho!"

■ **A Sheepherder**

One time I bought a Model T, and I drove it from Miami across the state of Arizona. You know that Arizona is pure, pure, pure desert. There I was, drunk. For me there was no such thing as roads, hills, or arroyos. I'd drive up a hill and go right down it. By sunset, I was already back in town. And I said to the wife:

"Tomorrow I'm going to California in my car. I'll be back by sunset."

"Oh no, you're not."

"Yes, I am. Why shouldn't I go?"

"But you won't make it back by sunset. The sun travels like the wind."

Next day I filled up the car with gasoline, really, really full. As soon as daylight broke—the sun rose—I headed for Indio, California. There I was, going through the desert. There were no roads. By the time it was ten or eleven o'clock, when the noon sun was about to hit, my car was already missing from the heat and all.

I spotted a sheepherder far off in the distance with his sheep. I said to myself, "I'm going to see how far it is to Indio."

Well, I headed over in that direction. I said to him:

"Listen! What's up?"

"Taking care of the sheep."

I looked around and then I said to him:

"How much farther before I get to Indio?" (literally, "How much more before turning into an Indian?")

"Listen!" he said to me. "The only thing you need is feathers!"

Lucinda Atencio
Bernalillo, NM

■ Saint Anthony

This boy lived with his father. The boy was already grown up, and one day his father says to him,

"Go ask Saint Anthony to help you find a job."

Okay. He took off for the church and there said his prayers. Then he said to him—to the large statue of Saint Anthony:

"Listen here, Saint Anthony! You had better find me a job. If not, I'm going to come cut you up."

And the priest, who was behind Saint Anthony, heard everything. The boy then took off, and the priest came and removed the large Saint Anthony and put in its place a small Saint Anthony statue. Next day the boy came back and said to him:

"Hey, Junior, where's your father?"

■ The Rag

There was this woman and her son. The mother was on her way to go visit her husband near the cemetery where he was working. Nearby there was a very mean little dog. No sooner had she left then she dropped her bandana (*la garra*), and the boy, her son, hollered at her:

"Mom, *la garra, la garra*" (a play on words, for the boy was calling attention to his mother because she dropped the bandana [*la garra*], but she misinterpreted *la 'garra* to mean "the dog's about to catch you").

The mother took off running like all get out. When she got to the cemetery fence, the boy, who had been following her, said to her:

"Now why did you run, Mom?"

"Why, you told me that that mean little dog was about to catch me!"

The Lean Bone

This woman is said to have been a real cutup. I understand that whenever her husband left home she would hang a lean bone outside the door, you know, so that her lover would know her husband wasn't home. One time I understand she forgot to take in the lean bone, and the husband came home from work. A short while later there was a terrible racket at the door. She said to him:

"Well, I don't know. Someone must have died. I guess they came to inform us. They're spirits. They're spirits."

"Yes," so the husband responded. "Well, pray to them. I'm already fed up with that racket."

"Okay" she responded.

You, my grieving spirit, I'll be the one to forgive you.

My husband's at home now, I forgot all about the lean bone.

There she was, praying so beautifully to the spirits. The dumb old man (her husband) fell for it.

The Sardines

This man didn't know English and he showed the cashier by holding his nose that what he wanted were sardines. Then the cashier said to him:

"Me don't know," until the man finally grabbed the cashier by the shoulder and told him to smell.

"Oh, you mean sardines! Yes, yes, sardines," he said after smelling his fingers (he had just eaten sardines), but at first the cashier didn't know what he wanted, because the man didn't know how to say sardines in English.

■ The Two Comadres

This compadre came knocking at the door. There he was knocking, but the comadres wouldn't pay attention to him.

"Don't open, comadre. Don't open."

"Open the door for me. I'm freezing, freezing to death."

"Don't open, comadre. He's drunk as a skunk."

"Comadre, comadre, open the door. I'm frozen stiff, frozen stiff."

"Open the door for him, comadre. He's got something stiff!"

■ The Baby Chicks

This man went and removed this setting hen and propped himself on the eggs. There they were, the baby chicks hatching. They were being born, one by one.

"There it comes. There it comes," so he said.

There he was on top of the eggs until all of the chicks hatched. Then he got up and here comes the hen and pecked at him.

"Nothing doing. Why, these baby chicks are mine! I hatched them. I hatched them."

He didn't let the hen come close to where the baby chicks were. Well, he finally got to keep the chicks. He hatched them. So he kept them. Later on, he went around telling people that he had hatched the chicks. He was a little off his rocker.

■ A Bowl Full of Gold

This is the story about an Indian and two rich men. They were eating at a table, and the Indian wanted to eat—he was hungry—but they wouldn't call to him. They wouldn't invite him. Then he headed their way, and he stopped and said to them:

"Listen, gentlemen, how much (food) are you willing to give for a bowl full of gold?"

"Come and eat! Pull up a chair! Come!"

The Indian ate. When he was full, he said to them:

"I now go."

"Where's the bowl of gold?"

"When I find it, when I find it."

Elba C. de Baca
Las Vegas, NM

■ To Saragosa

One day a crow ran into his friend the parrot. The crow says to him:
"Good morning, Parrot. I'm in a hurry, headed for Saragosa."
Perico answered:
"Hello, Crow. You shall go to Saragosa, God willing!"
Responded the crow:
"I'm going whether God likes it or not!"
Well, the crow took off flying when all of a sudden a terrible earthquake struck and knocked him into a deep hole.
The following month the crow ran into the parrot. The parrot said to him:
"Where are you going in such a hurry?"
"Oh," says the crow. "I'm going to Saragosa or a deep hole!"

■ Two Hippies

One day two hippies were walking through the woods chatting. One of them says to the other:
"Do you know what happened? I was reading that the Holy Father fell in the bathtub and broke a leg."
Asked the other hippie:
"Well, what's a bathtub?"
The hippie answers:
"How should I know? I'm not Catholic!"

■ The Moon and the Cat

The moon says to the little cat:

"So small and with a mustache!"

The little cat answered:

"And what about you, who's not at all ashamed to spend all night long looking at everything that's none of your business!"

■ Did You Also Buy Wood?

One day a wood seller came to a house where there was a parrot, alone. The wood seller hollered:

"Do you want to buy wood?"

The parrot answered him from inside the house:

"Yes, just dump it there!"

When the owner returned, he got very mad at the parrot. That afternoon the owner started to scold his son for being a bad little boy. The son started crying. Hollered the parrot:

"Did you also buy wood?"

■ You, My Lady, Choose

Juan and Justo headed for the dance. A short while later a young lady named Tila arrived at the dance, along with a friend. Tila was lame. Juan says to Justo:

"I bet you won't go to Tila and taunt her about being lame."

Answered Justo:

"And why not! Come with me and I'll show you."

Juan and Justo then went to Tila, and Justo offered her a rose and says to her:

"Take this flower or this rose, my dear young lady you be the one to choose." (*Escoja* means to choose, but the play on words denotes "you're lame"—*es coja*.)

Alfonso Cantú
Manassa, CO

■ A Bit Off His Rocker

One time there were these two brothers. One was named Juan and the other José. Juan was a little bit off his rocker. One day his brother José asked him to go buy a pair of gloves with the blue leather trimming. So Juan took off and got to the store. The cashiers were Americans (Anglos), and one of them says to him:

"What you want?"

"Yes, *guante* (glove)," Juan answers.

"What you say?" the clerk says to him.

"Yes, for José," Juan replies.

"Oh, you fool!"

"Yes, those with the leather trimming *azul* (blue)."

"Oh, you go to hell!" the clerk responds.

"Yes, that's what José wanted you to sell me," says Juan.

Then the cashier got mad. He couldn't understand him, so he chased him off.

Felipe Cantú
Manassa, CO

■ The Mexican Who Thought He Knew English

There were these two men, an American (Anglo) and a Mexican. And the Mexican didn't know a word of English. The story goes that the Mexican told his wife:

"Now I'm really going to make an effort to speak English."

Then his wife said to him:

"Whenever they ask you a question you say *yes*."

Later on an American ran into him, and the American says:

"Do you want to fight?"

The Mexican then responds *yes*, and he (the American) beats the heck out of him. He then goes and tells his wife that the American had beaten the tar out of him.

"Well, next time you say *no* to him," says the wife.

Once again he ran into the American, and the latter says to him:

"Did you have enough?"

"No," says the Mexican, and the American gave him another good beating.

■ An Argument

There were these three men, a lawyer, a doctor, and a shepherd. They were in a heated argument as to who would last longer locked up in a room with a skunk. Well, the lawyer went in first and lasted five minutes. Next came the doctor. He lasted about fifteen minutes. The shepherd entered last, but the skunk finally left the room because he couldn't stand the smell of the shepherd.

José Ignacio Cantú
Manassa, CO

■ The Married Couple

If it's true, the truth will come out; if it's a lie, the same thing applies. Well, this man and this woman got married. They were married by a priest. And as you know, a holy matrimony by a priest must always be obeyed. That's why they were being respectful. But the marriage turned sour. And so the husband said to the wife:

"If we're not to live happily, it's best to go our separate ways."

"Okay," she says to him, "but we'll have to go see the priest so he can annul the marriage."

They took off to see the priest. They got there and told the priest that they wanted to annul their marriage since they no longer wished to live together.

"Very well," said the priest, "come back tomorrow all dressed the same as the day you got married so that I can annul the marriage."

They returned to see the priest. The priest was already at the steps to the altar in his vestments prepared to "unmarry" them. And he grabbed the censer in one hand while he talked to them, but at the same time striking them with the censer, first one and then the other—hitting them a little harder with each succeeding blow. Toward the end he began hitting them in the face, and then one started to bleed, then the other. So the wife says to the priest:

"Well, what is it that you're going to do with us?"

"I'm going to kill one of you," said the priest.

"No, you're not," responded the wife, "for it's better to live together than for one of us to be dead."

"Well, there's no other way to separate one from the other," said the priest.

Thus they repented, left the church, and went to live happily together.

35

Adrián Chávez
Armijo (Albuquerque), NM

■ Two Priests

Once there were these two priests, and one of them was quite a drinker. He loved liquor. At times he didn't even know he was drunk, but at any rate, he always went to visit his pal, quite frequently, in fact. On one of his trips he gave up drinking.

Well, one morning he took off to mail a letter but didn't know where the post office was. On up ahead he ran into a little boy, so the priest talked to him:

"Listen, my good child," he says to him. "Where's the post office around here?"

"Well, over there, a few blocks up ahead."

Out of the clear blue sky, the priest said to him:

"And why didn't you go to school today?"

"Well, you see, because of this and that."

The priest started to give him advice:

"Listen, my dear son," he says to him. "You had better go to school; it's very important. Are you a Christian?"

"Yes and no."

"You better think more about that," he says to the child, "so that good children such as yourself are better acquainted with the road to heaven."

"Well said! But for someone like you who has prayed so much," said the child to the priest, "how come you don't even know the way to the post office?"

Filiberto Esquibel
Cañada del Medio, NM

■ The Cholesterol

I'm going to tell you a very simple joke. You know how some people have high cholesterol? There was this little old man. He was very heavy. And his wife said to him:

"You can barely breathe. Let's go to the doctor. You better go. Let's go."

And she took him with her. She went and spoke with the doctor. She spoke better English than he did. She told the doctor what it was she wanted. The husband sat in the waiting room. Then the doctor called the little old man, and he said to him:

"Let me examine you. It's for your own good."

Yes, the cholesterol was very high. And the doctor said to him:

"What do you eat for breakfast?"

"I put down about four eggs."

"Aha! That's where the problem lies," he said to him, and he called the wife. "Listen here, you have got to cut this man's eggs (*huevos* is also balls) in the morning."

Next morning the little old lady came out with a knife.

"What in the devil are you going to do with that knife?"

"Well, this is what the doctor asked me to do," she answered.

"Tell the doctor that he's asking too much. You're not going to touch me with that knife!"

■ Gene Autry

There were these two musicians, and one said to the other:

"Do you know what happened to Gene Autry? The Indians captured him and tied him to a pine tree. They started to gather dry wood. And Gene Autry went and hollered at his horse, Champion."

His horse went to run an errand as he was told. He took off running. He didn't even take half an hour. He came back really fast with a naked woman, close to Gene Autry where he was tied. A very beautiful woman. Very shapely. And Gene Autry slapped his horse on the face. He says to his horse:

"I sent you for a posse, not a pussy!"

Félix Esquivel
San Pablo, CO

■ The Man with the Calf

A New Mexican was on his way to California, and he came to this house where two men were eating, but they didn't invite him to join them. And one of them said to him:

"What's it like where you come from?"

"Oh, it's a huge country, a very rich country!"

"What kinds of riches are there?"

"So much wealth that when all of the families in New Mexico eat, they use a small spoon with each bite."

The two men were astounded to hear that for each bite there was a tiny spoon, but the man didn't tell them that the tiny spoon was the tortilla.

"Besides that," he said to them, "the cows over where I come from are not like those here."

"Why not?"

"Because those here only give birth to one calf, and those in my country give birth to two at a time."

"And how do they manage to nurse the two calves?"

"Easy, just like you two now. While one eats (nurses), the other one watches."

■ The Boy Who Wanted to Marry His Grandmother

This man had a young son of about four years old, and he says to his father:

"Dad, when I grow up, will I be able to marry my grandmother?"

"Watch it there, you little rascal! And why do you want to marry my mother?"

"Wait a minute!" says the boy. "How come you married mine?"

■ The Young Man Who Didn't Invite His Parents

This is the story about a young man who asked for a girl's hand in marriage, and her parents set a wedding date. He started to invite his friends. One of his friends, seeing that he (the young man) was not inviting his own parents to the wedding, asked him why not. The young man, sighing, responded:

"Because my feelings are hurt. When they got married, they didn't invite me."

Carmelita Gómez
Aguilar, NM

■ My Uncle Pedro Had a Very Hoarse Voice

My grandma had a brother, and he was kind of a smart aleck. Back about that time, he went around talking about the bogeyman, this and that. I understand my grandma said to him.

"Listen. Shut up!"

"What?" he asked.

He was very hoarse. My Uncle Pedro had a very hoarse voice. I understand he told her that he was going to say the Our Father. Instead of saying Our Father, he said Fart Father. And she burst out laughing.

■ Bread Made of Dung

I had a very prankish granddaughter, there in Rincón de las Mujeres. One time we went over to Rincón at a place called Jorupa. Let me tell you something. That's where we had crops—chile and everything. We had a lot of vegetables planted in Jorupa. Lots of things grew there, and Crescencio, my husband, said to me:

"Why don't you take along some flour?"

And he set up an iron grill. Do you know what an iron grill is? On top of it is where he placed the live coals to bake the bread. Then he said to me:

"Go tell your mom to knead some dough."

So Mom went and made the dough while Crescencio built the fire. He fed the fire cow chips. Cow dung. Then next day Presila, my granddaughter, went and said to her teacher, Juan Padilla:

"Listen!" she said. "My grandpa knows how to bake bread with dung."

"How so?"

"Why yes," she said to him. "He put the cow chips on top of the grill to bake bread."

She went and told the teacher. As a result a bunch of boys went over to the house because they wanted to see the dung bread in Jorupa. But that Presila was something else.

Basilio Gonzales
Gonzales Ranch, NM

■ Why Did You Kill My Dog?

One time this dog had bitten one of our cows. I felt like shooting him. It so happened that a cousin of mine and I were at the corner of our house, and I said to him:

"There's that dog and I don't even have bullets."

"I have some," he said.

He had some with him. He stuck his hand in his pocket to grab some while I went and got the .22. I took a shot at the dog near the dam, there close to the road.

Well, then my godfather showed up. The dog belonged to my godfather. He came here to the house and said to me:

"Why did you fire a shot at my dog?"

"I didn't fire at your dog."

"Well, someone took a shot at him. Someone wounded him."

"I don't know who shot him," I responded.

"Okay," said my godfather, and he took off.

He went to where the other boy was. He was a cousin of mine. He went and said to him:

"Why did you kill my dog?"

"I haven't killed your dog," answered my cousin.

"Well, Basilio said that you had killed him because the bullet is yours."

"Basilio is a liar! He killed it. All I did was loan him the bullet, but he killed it, because the rifle is his," he said to him.

But no, nothing happened to the dog. The only thing is that my godfather wanted to scare us. Later on my cousin and I just laughed about it. But I guess my godfather was pretty shrewd because he went and told my cousin that I had killed it.

■ Corn Is Like a Lie!

One time Dad and I were planting corn. We used to plant it by hand. I had about a five-pound can and so as to finish quickly. I poured out the corn in a row from one end to the other. My dad said to me:

"Do you know something, my son? Corn is like a lie!"

I didn't pay much attention. I knew very well what he meant. Well, when the corn came out (sprouted), he took me over to see it.

"Do you remember what I told you, my son?" he said to me. "Look and see if corn isn't like a lie."

The corn came out all bunched up where I had planted it. Just like a lie. I guess if you tell a lie, one way or another, at some future time, it comes out.

Reynaldo Gonzales
Los Juertes, NM

■ My First Car

I don't even want to think about that car, my first car. I bought that car from my wife's father. Then the car, well, man, it was in very bad shape. I traded it for another car. It was also a very old car.

But I always had mules and horses. Well, so as not to bring the two horses to climb this steep hill, because the road was pretty bad, I would hitch up one of the mules to the front of the car. I would talk to the mule to pull, to help the car, while I drove it. Well, this mule didn't know anything. She was terrible. Real dense. Time and again, I scolded the mule until I taught her what to do. She finally learned what to do. I'd put the harness on and hitch her behind the car until we got to the place where the car started having trouble climbing. Then I'd hitch the mule to the front of the car. I would command the mule to pull, to help me with the car, while I drove it. Whenever the mule didn't understand, well, I'd give her a few hard whacks. I would even throw stones at it or give it a few good swats, and then she would climb the steep hill.

After that I would remove the harness and put it in the back of the car. The mule then went back to the house. As for the car, I kept it for a while. It was already my second car.

Then there were these teachers who went to teach over at the ranch. They used to pay for someone to bring them here to Las Vegas. They had to come to get paid or to buy groceries. And this lady, a young girl, asked me to bring her, so I did. The car by now was already quite old. The cab was made of cloth, and it was already rotten. Well, when we were returning from here in Las Vegas to the ranch, a storm caught us on the way back. There I was and I had that girl with me, the teacher, plus another girl. You know how it is, these women bought dishes and who knows what else. Well, the car top leaked, and so they put the baking pans or bowls on top of their heads so as not to get wet.

But I took them back. And that ends the story about my cars. "No more," I said to myself. "No, no more cars. No more putting up with cars." I went and bought my first truck!

Francisco Herrera
Antoñito, CO

■ The Cowboy

There was this cowboy who wanted to marry this girl, but the girl didn't like him, and he didn't know how to convince her to marry him.

Finally, he got this man to go with him to see the girl. And whenever he said that he had something, the man was to say that it was much larger than what it was. When they got to the girl's house, the cowboy began telling her all that he owned. He told her that he had a little ranch, and the other man says:

"Not just a little ranch, a humongous ranch!"

And he told her that he had a little house, and the other man says:

"Not just a little house, a huge house. A palace!"

The cowboy then says to the girl that he's got a few cows, and the other man says that they're huge herds of cattle, not just a few head. Then the cowboy tells the girl that he's got a few sheep, and his companion says:

"Not just a few sheep, huge flocks of sheep!"

"I have a few horses."

"Not just a few horses, huge herds of horses."

There he was, the cowboy, telling the girl all that he owned, and she became increasingly interested in him. But she noticed that he wasn't comfortable sitting down, so she says to him:

"Sit down, relax, sir."

"Why, I can't," said the cowboy. "I have these tiny sores from riding horseback."

Responded his traveling companion:

"Not just tiny sores, humongous sores! He's rotten."

And right then and there the girl lost interest, and she refused to marry him.

Fred W. Korte
Buena Vista/Las Vegas, NM

■ Two Men Crossing a Desert

One man says to the other:

"Wait just a little bit for me. I have to go do my business."

He went behind a sagebrush. He dropped his pants, and about that time a snake sneaked up and bit him right in his butt.

He calls his friend and says to him:

"Oh, what a pain, my friend! Do something for me!"

Answers his friend:

"I don't know how to cure snakebites."

Answers his friend:

"Then go quickly to town and tell a doctor that I'm in agony with grave pain from the snakebite."

Quickly he went galloping to town and saw a doctor. He told the doctor all about what had happened and asked him what he could do for his friend. The doctor responded:

"There's only one thing you can do. Sharpen your knife on a rock and make two incisions like so, in the shape of a cross, and suck the venom with your mouth."

He returned quickly and as he was arriving, his friend kept asking him rather anxiously:

"What did the doctor say? What did the doctor say?"

"Well, the doctor told me that there's no cure for you. That you just have to die!"

■ The Cellular Phone

A man received a cellular phone for Christmas. He liked it so much that he used it all day long and at night he even took it to bed with him.

One day he telephoned his doctor and informed him that he was very sick and couldn't go see him, but for him to send some medicine for his arthritic pain. The doctor told him to collect one week's urine specimen in a bedpan and for him to send it with his wife. In that way, he would be able to do an analysis and thus decide on the medicine best suited for him.

For a whole week he collected his specimen in a bedpan, and since he always carried the phone with him, he accidently dropped the phone in the bedpan. He retrieved it quickly and dried it clean. He thought that his phone no longer worked, but it continued working as always. He was very happy.

By the end of the week his wife was on her way to take the bedpan full of specimen to the doctor. She took a shortcut through a fence where there were some cows. With this shortcut instead of five miles to the village there were only three.

When she started crossing the fence, she accidently stumbled on a rock and lost almost all of the specimen. She became very worried because her husband was going to get mad at her. Just at that very moment she saw a young steer urinating. She went and filled the bedpan.

This was the specimen that she took to the doctor.

Two weeks later the doctor called him with the report. He told him that he was quite confused with the results, for in all the years of practicing medicine he had never had a case such as his. He added:

"Why, I even checked up to six or seven times, and the results are the same. There is no doubt about it! You are pregnant with a telephone but are going to give birth to a young steer."

Anastasio Lobato
Antoñito, CO

■ The Three Gachupíns

There once were these three *gachupíns* (low-class Spaniards) who went to a city to learn to speak Spanish. They were there a long time, but one was only able to say "we," the second one "because we wanted to," and the third one, "it's only fair."

One night there was some entertainment on the plaza, and a man was murdered. The three men got scared and took off running. The one who knew how to say "it's only fair" was ahead of the others. The one who knew how to say "because we wanted to" was in the middle, and the one who knew how to say "we" was farther back. The authorities then went after them. When they caught up with the first one, they asked him who had murdered the man, and he responded:

"We (did)."

Then the friend who was in the middle showed up, and they said to him:

"Why?"

"Because we wanted to," said he.

"Then we must kill all three of you," said the authorities.

"It's only fair," said the other.

Edumenio Lovato
San Luis, NM

■ It Rained Something Terrible

I'm going to tell you a story that my grandfather used to tell. I don't know if you want to hear it or not. Well, one time, long ago, when it was very dry, there was lots of wheat, and it was drying up. People didn't have any water, and they went and took out the Holy Child. The Holy Child of Atocha was a very special devotion of mine when I was young. And the people took Him out in a procession. Back in those days, people would take Him to the fields to show Him how the fields were drying up.

Well, that night after they prayed to Him and everything, it rained something terrible. And it flooded all of the wheat fields; it flooded all of the sown fields. The rain left them flattened.

Well, the following day the people, the old folks, snubbed Him, and they proceeded to take out the Holy Mother of Jesus. They took Her out—and they said to Her: "We want you to see the shitty mess that your son made yesterday after we begged Him for rain."

Salomón Lovato
San Luis, NM

■ Why Don't You Put the Santos Out to Hoe?

That Virgin sitting there that I showed you, when (Bernardino) Jovey went to the war—that was World War I—his mother punished Her. She kept Her in the footlocker until She brought him back.

And a lot of people, the Holy Child more than anyone else, they'd punish Him. People would say: "I put the Holy Child in such and such a place," and it wasn't there. It'd show up somewhere else. They'd punish the santos.

Also, when they sowed the fields, they'd put Saint Anthony or Saint Isidore at the threshing ground. One day an uncle of mine, he was already up in years, he was a humorous man, told someone, I don't remember who:

"Did you put the santos over there?"

"Yes," said the man, "'cause there's a terrible drought!"

"Why don't you put the santos out to hoe instead? The weeds are taking over!" said my uncle.

■ The Priest Didn't Want My Five Dollars

One time we were celebrating the fiestas at Cabezón, and a friend of mine was there whose name is Avenicio Maestas. He now lives in San Ysidro. And there was a priest, Father Leonardo—a great big German! He was rough! And Avenicio was in Mass when the priest passed the collection plate.

The poor thing didn't have any change, but he handed the priest five dollars and said to him:

"Señor, sir, my friend wants to know if you'll sell him this barrel."
And the gringo says to him:
"I don't know. I don't know."
Then the man goes back and tells his friend:
"He says that he'll sell you the barrel but the metal bands no."
"What? Why would I want a barrel with no bands?"

■ A Job

This is the story about two gentlemen who came from Mexico. They were looking for work. They were musicians. They got to Denver. There, they went from here to there with their violin and guitar, so they hopped on the streetcar. The manager—the conductor—comes up to them and says:

"Token (*toquen*, pronounced the same way, means "play"), please."

"What a stroke of luck, my friend! We have found ourselves a job," and they started playing.

■ My Sister-in-Law

My sister-in-law used to tell the story about not being able to speak English. And one day the little girl who sat behind her in school fainted. Then my sister-in-law says to the sister, the nun, the teacher:

"Sister, sister! She's smiled, she's smiled! (*Se desmayó* in Spanish for "she fainted" sounds like "she smiled").

And the sister says:

"That's nice."

"No, no. She smiled."

Finally the nun realized that the little girl had fainted.

That's How She Spoke English

There was this woman who always went to visit my mother. She was always carrying on about, "The old man, sheck and sheck it!" ("shake and shake it!"). That's how she spoke English because she didn't how to speak it. She'd say to the old man:

"Sheck and sheck it!"

And the old man would say,

"Lift up your dress and take it."

What they were doing was gathering apples, but people thought they were doing something else.

The Deaf Man

This man came by on foot, asking for lodging. He came to this house and asked for lodging. He knocked on the door, and this woman says to him:

"Yes, we'll put you up for the night. You'll have to sleep on the floor, but it's cold and we'll give you something to eat," she said. "The only thing is that my husband's very deaf. You're going to have to speak very, very loud so he can hear you."

So she introduced him to her husband, and the man seeking lodging said to them:

"Thank you very much, thank you very much for the lodging."

Very well then. They chatted for a little bit. They ate supper and went to bed. And they retired early as was the custom long ago. Then the man who sought lodging knelt down and began to pray. And he said (speaking to the wife):

"When the deaf man has fallen asleep and you sense that he's sound asleep, get up from your bed and come and hop in bed with me. And don't you forget, and don't you forget."

And the deaf man says to the wife:

"Look, my dear, what a wonderful Christian!"

Cruz Márquez
Conejos, CO

■ The Two Ranchers

There were these two ranchers, José María and Antonio. They lived close to each other, and both raised animals and sold butter, eggs, meat, and milk. The two ranchers called each other compadre. One time these Americans (Anglos) showed up. José María knew absolutely no word of English. The Americans asked him to sell them some eggs and milk. He did his best to make himself understood using sign language. One of the Americans then told him that they were going to sleep on the other side of the small river and for him to go collect his due next day. Well, not knowing English, he says to his wife:

"I'm going to go see my compadre so he can interpret for me. He knows English very well."

So he takes off and goes to see his compadre, and he says to him:

"I came to tell you that yesterday afternoon these two Americans stopped by the house and they bought milk and eggs from me. We did our best to understand each other, and they said that they were going to sleep on the other side of the river and that's where they are. Now I want you to go with me to act as my interpreter."

"Very well," says Don Antonio. "Let's go."

When they get there, Don Antonio says to the Americans:

"Gur morning, *gringos ladrones. Al pay mi compadre* José María. You *no al pay mi compadre* José María. I'll breque your neque *con un palo esteque.*"

Well, the American couldn't understand, but he finally paid him. On the way back, Don José María says to Don Antonio:

"If it hadn't been for you, the Americans wouldn't have paid me."

"I know English perfectly," says Don Antonio. "I'm not at all embarrassed to speak it."

Benerito Seferino Martínez
Trujillo, CO/Farmington, NM

■ Don Cacahuate and Doña Cebolla

Don Cacahuate and Doña Cebolla once upon a time were very poor. They didn't have any money. They didn't have money for anything, and Doña Cebolla kept trying his patience because she wanted to go traveling, but they were penniless. Finally Don Cacahuate got tired of listening to her and he said to her:

"Okay, let's go make the rounds."

And she says to him:

"How are we going? How are we going to pay? Why, we don't have any money. We have nothing with which to pay."

And he answers her:

"Don't sweat it. It's not going to cost anything. The fare (passage) is free."

"And how are we going to go?" Doña Cebolla asked him.

"Well, wait just a minute, I'll tell you."

And so they got their lunch and knapsacks and everything ready. They headed by way of the railroad tracks. There they were down the railroad tracks. Then she said to him:

"Didn't you say we were going to go traveling?"

"Yes, here we are. Here we are traveling."

"Didn't you also say that we were going to go an easy way?" said she.

"Yes, here we are going the easy way. Down the railroad tracks, just like the train."

And Doña Cebolla says to him:

"Didn't you also say that we don't have any money? How are we going to pay for the train fare?"

"Don't worry about it, my dear. Nobody's charging you anything to walk down the tracks!"

■ The Motorcycle

One time Don Cacahuate and Doña Cebolla were also very poor, and they didn't have any means of transportation. Finally—I don't know how it came about—but he bought himself a motorcycle. There he was showing off as he headed home to show Doña Cebolla the motorcycle. And he says to her:

"Let's take a drive down the road."

Since cars had come out about that time, they were on the road along with motorcycles. Back then the roads were not very wide. There was no room to pass a car, so Doña Cebolla finally said:

"Okay, I'll go for a ride with you."

There they were on the road, and it got dark on them. Then Don Cacahuate went and turned on the motorcycle light. There they were riding along very smugly in their air-conditioned motorcycle. Well, all of a sudden they see two lights in the distance coming toward them, and he says to her:

"Just watch what I'm going to do, Doña Cebolla. I'm going to go right between those two motorcycles, and I'm going to scare the wits out of them."

And the lights kept getting closer and closer, until Don Cacahuate finally said:

"Are you set? Ready? Here I go between the two motorcycles."

When all of a sudden, bang! It was a car. Not two motorcycles!

■ Ice Cream

When Don Cacahuate was young, he went in the military, to war. It took him four or five years to return. And since there were no telephones or mail or television, Doña Cebolla didn't have any news about Don Cacahuate, who was at war in the military. After four or five years, Don Cacahuate came home, and by then Doña Cebolla already had a little boy four or five years old.

Okay, everything went all right at first, and then Don Cacahuate asked her:

"Listen, Doña Cebolla. That child, where did he come from?"

"Well, let me tell you, Don Cacahuate. Since you weren't here, I bought ice cream, and I ate ice cream, and that's where he came from, for sure."

One day Don Cacahuate decided that he was going to go trout fishing, and he said to Doña Cebolla:

"I believe I'll take the little boy, the ice cream boy, so he can learn how to fish."

And Doña Cebolla says:

"Ah, why of course. He has to learn how to catch trout."

Very well. Don Cacahuate took off fishing in the morning with the little boy. He returned in the evening with the trout and yellow-belly suckers that they had caught, but the little boy didn't return home. Finally, curiosity got the best of Doña Cebolla.

"Don Cacahuate, what happened to my son? Where is he? Why didn't he return with you?"

And Don Cacahuate responded:

"Well, let me tell you, Doña Cebolla. Since he was made of ice cream, and being that it was so hot and there was so much sun, he melted!"

■ The Mirror

Okay, then. Don Cacahuate and Doña Cebolla had a son. The poor son was drafted into the military service. Back then there weren't very many things available. Many things were still being invented. Over where he was stationed, he saw a mirror and he said to himself, "Well, we don't have one of these in our house. We have to go to the river to look at ourselves. I'm going to buy it and send it home."

Finally, some two or three years after the son had been in the service, they received the mirror. Don Cacahuate's the one who picked it up at the post office. When he got home, Doña Cebolla said to him:

"Well, open the package to see what's in it."

Don Cacahuate then started to open the package. He finally got it opened. There he was looking at it (the mirror), and he started crying. Doña Cebolla kept saying:

"Well, why are you crying? Why are you crying? Why are you crying?"

And Don Cacahuate said:

"Oh, poor thing! Well, I'm crying for my son. Look how old he looks."

And finally Doña Cebolla says to him:

"Well, what did our son send, a photograph or what? Why are you crying, because he's gotten so old? Come. Give me that picture."

Why no. Then Doña Cebolla saw the mirror and got angry at Don Cacahuate.

"And for this so and so . . . ," and she let off a few cuss words. "And you're shedding tears over this bitch?"

■ Denver Bound

When Don Cacahuate and Doña Cebolla lived in Mexico, they were also very poor. Finally they decided, "If we move, we can have a better life." They thought and thought, until one day Don Cacahuate says to Doña Cebolla:

"What do you say we move to Denver?"

And she says:

"Well, I don't even know where Denver's located!"

"I don't know either. I don't know where Denver might be situated, but we'll go by the map, we'll follow the road," he says to her.

Very well, then. Everything started off just fine. They came through El Paso and from there on to Las Cruces, Albuquerque, and Española, until they got to Colorado. There they went, extremely happy saying "We're almost there." They had all of their furniture loaded on the small truck they had bought for the move. They got to Colorado Springs. Everything was going along just fine. They saw a sign that read, "Denver, 100 miles." They got very happy and started to sing: "El Rancho Grande," "La Cucaracha," and so forth. They were singing, very happy indeed.

Well, they were getting closer, and they saw a sign that read 50 miles and then 25, and then 10, and then 5, and still very happy. There they were going down the road in the little truck full of furniture when Don Cacahuate saw a sign, and he pulled to the side of the road. He stopped the little truck and started crying. Doña Cebolla didn't know what was going on, so she kept asking him:

"Don Cacahuate, Don Cacahuate, why are you crying?"

Doña Cebolla, being that she didn't know how to read, was trying to console him and at the same time asking him "Why are you crying?" so that Don Cacahuate would answer her, but he couldn't say anything. There he was crying, wiping the drivel off his mouth along with his tears, while at the same time trying to catch his breath. And he kept pointing to the sign for Doña Cebolla, but she didn't know how to read. And the poor thing kept on crying, crying, crying, until finally, in between sighs, he was able to tell her:

"Denver has gone."

And Doña Cebolla says to him:

"You know very well that I can't speak or read English. What does that sign mean? What does it say?"

And he answers:

"We messed up, Doña Cebolla."

"Why?" she asks.

"Because it says, 'Denver Left.' Denver has left. In other words, we won't be able to find it."

Estefanita Q. Martínez
De Tierra (Gonzales Ranch), NM

■ Who killed the Rooster?

Now let me tell you. Don Julián and Doña Conchita had just arrived at my grandma's house, and Grandma said to me:

"Stay out of the way, sweet one! Go sit down! Go outside and play."

Back then they didn't let you walk in front of people (guests) as they do now. Then I said to her:

"Okay, I'll go in a little bit," but I walked in front of the people just the same. Said my grandmother:

"As soon as the guests leave, we're going to eat the rooster. You're going to get it!"

I went outside very happy thinking about it. I sat down under some small pine trees that were near the house. Then I said to myself: "Well, my grandma said that she wanted rooster for supper. I'm going to kill the rooster. By the time the people leave, it will be ready." I got him inside the chicken coop, and I wrung his neck until I killed it. I took it to my aunt and told her that my grandma wanted to eat rooster as soon as the people left. Then my poor aunt took the rooster to a small room (dispensary), plucked its feathers, and put them underneath a tin tub.

I stayed outside showing off until the people left. Then my grandma said to my aunt:

"Get her in here! What was going on with the rooster? This disobedient little brat is going to get it."

I went and fetched the rooster from the room that she (my aunt) had put it in and took it to her. I said:

"Here it is, look, so that we can have meat for supper!"

She turned around, looked at me, and said:

"Come here! What were you doing? Who killed the rooster?"

"When I walked in front of the guests you said to me, 'As soon as the people leave we're going to eat rooster.'"

I, the stupid fool, went and killed her rooster. And I couldn't keep from laughing! My grandma also cracked up. She said to my aunt:

"Cook it! Put it in the oven! And don't dilly dally!"

Well, as soon as the people left, we ate meat (the rooster). And do you know that my grandma didn't do anything to me? I saved myself from a good beating.

Cesaria Montoya
San Pablo, NM

■ Between You and an Idiot, There's Little Difference

Well, as far as good jokes go, I can't recall a single one. Only dirty jokes! It's best not even to tell them because . . .

One time this man was on horseback, and this other man, a little old fellow, was hoeing his corn, that is what he had planted. And the man on horseback stopped by and said to him:

"Good morning (May God grant you a good day)."

"Good morning."

"What is it you're doing?"

"Here I am, hoeing my little cornfield."

"My, but it's dry," the rider commented. "Why is it so yellow? Why is the corn so yellow?"

"Because it was yellow corn that I planted."

The man on horseback started to ask things like that, and the little old man began responding in kind until the man riding the horse said to him:

"Oh," he said to him, "between you and an idiot, there's very little difference."

"Yes, that's right," said the little old man. "Only the fence stands in the way!"

Filimón Montoya
Cañón de Fernández (Taos), NM

■ Don Cacahuate

Well, Don Cacahuate and Doña Cebolla were not a couple as such. They didn't have a family. But they went from town to town. They traveled about in their tattered clothes and their knapsacks draped over their shoulders.

"And we're going to go by rail," he told her.

And Doña Cebolla understood that they were going to go by train. Don Cacahuate added:

"Because I have free passage."

He didn't clarify for her that they were going to go on foot down the railroad tracks.

"By rail," he said to her.

But she misunderstood. Off they went so that by noon Doña Cebolla was quite tired. She said to him:

"Listen here, Don Cacahuate! Didn't you say that you had free passage?"

"So, who's charging you, lady?"

José Nataleo Montoya
San Pablo, NM

■ Prudencio Santillanes

There was a fellow named Prudencio Santillanes. That was his name. He was one of these so-called liars, but he was like someone on television, you get it? As an excuse to listen to him, well, people would gather around to hear the lies that he shared with them, you see?

One time, as far as I can recollect, from there in San Gerónimo he left for San Isidro. He left on a female donkey. Who knows what business he had or if he went just to make the rounds or something. Well, on his way back, the comadre in San Isidro sent her comadre here in San Gerónimo some cheese. He then tied this sack (of cheese), a little sack, to the saddle of the female donkey that he was riding. At a place called El Corral de Encino, where the road used to run years ago, somewhere along there, the cheese got caught on something. When he got home to San Gerónimo, his wife asked him:

"How did it go? How was your trip? Fine? How are my compadre and my comadre?"

"Why, they're fine. Oh, by the way," he says to her, "she sent you some cheese."

"Is that so?" she responded.

He then went to where the donkey was and found a thread (of cheese), like sewing thread.

"Look," he said to her. "Evidently this cheese got caught on something somewhere along the way."

Then he went and grabbed the strand between his fingers and proceeded to roll it into a small ball of cheese and retrace it until he reached Corral de Encino, where he finished rolling the thread into a ball of cheese.

■ She Can Go to Hell!

This is the story about Tomás. It so happened that he lost his wife, but while he lived with her he was very mean to her. He would beat her up and scold her and everything. He mistreated her in every way possible. And so she died, and he was left alone.

Well, his mind started playing tricks on him, and he said to himself, "Ah, I was so mean to my wife. I wonder how she's getting along? Perhaps she didn't even go to heaven, but I'm going to see if I can find someone who can help me get her to heaven."

Sure enough! There he was, going here and there until he found a woman who spoke to him. He found out that she was capable of helping him. So he went and consulted with her. They came to terms.

"Yes," she said to him, "I'll get her to heaven. All you have to do is bring me fifty dollars and come back in seven days."

Sure enough! He gave her fifty dollars and off he went. Seven days later he returned, and as soon as he saw her, he said:

"How's it going?"

"Oh, fine. Do you know that I already found her?"

"Really?"

"Yes, really."

"And how is she?"

"She's more or less fine, but she's still far from heaven."

"Then, what are we going to do to get her to heaven?"

"Well, bring me another fifty dollars and come back in seven days."

There she had him on a string. For quite some time she had him bring fifty dollars, returning seven days later, until one time he came and found this woman quite fatigued.

"What's wrong?"

"Ah!" she said to him. "I'm so tired. I've worked so much, but we're almost there. Your wife is but three feet away from the gates of heaven."

"Really?"

"Yes. It's really true."

"And now what are we going to do?"

"Well, give me another fifty dollars, and I'll get her into heaven."

"No way!" snapped the husband. "If she can't jump three feet, she can go straight to hell!"

Katarina Montoya
El Ojo (Taos), NM

■ Juan Cuchillete

There were two brothers, and one of them was very, very astute, and the king was the godfather of one of them, of Juan Cuchillete. He was the shrewd one. The other brother was younger. The king said to the younger one:

"You're going to stay with my mother today. You have to feed her blue corn gruel; don't let her go hungry. Be sure to give her enough."

Well, the boy was really stupid. He stuffed so much corn gruel down the little old lady's throat that he choked her to death. When Juan Cuchillete got home and found out about the king's mother, he said to his younger brother:

"Now let me tell you what we're going to do. We're going to fix her up real pretty, and we're going to stand her up against the door. Then you go and tell my godfather that I want to see him."

Well, the king went and when he opened the door, down went the little old lady. Right away Juan Cuchillete jumped up and said to the king:

"Look at what you've done to your mother! You've killed her!"

Francisco R. Mora
Wagon Mound/Ratón, NM

■ Belly Water

I ask ranchers if they've ever drunk belly water. And they say to me:
"No, we have never drunk belly water."
And I say to them:
"Yes, yes, you have."
The cowboy, but it doesn't have to be a cowboy, can be out in the
plains. He gets thirsty. And he wants to drink water, right? Fine, there's a
watering hole where the cows, coyotes, horses, and all the animals drink.
The water is a bit dirty, full of debris. And I say to the ranchers:
"All right. You have to drink water just as I do. You somehow have
to stoop down and somehow get down on your knees. On your belly."
I tell them that they have to drink water with their hands. The best
way is on your belly. You have to get down on the ground, near the watering hole, and slap on it with your hands. You have to remove all of the
cobwebs and all the junk that's in the watering hole. But you must do it
on your belly. That's why it's called belly water.

Rosie Mora
Springer/Ratón, NM

■ Doña Sebastiana

Centuries ago there was a married couple. The couple already had lots of little children and then one more was born. Well, they ran out of godparents. Everybody they knew was their co-parent. Then the husband said to the wife:

"I'm going to hit the road. And the first person I run into, whether it be a woman or a man, it doesn't matter, I'm going to ask that person to be a godparent," so he took off down the road.

When down the road a ways he ran into my co-mother Sebastiana (symbol of death).

"Oh, my lady! You're just the person I need to see."

"And why?"

"Because we have a newborn child, and we ran out of godparents. Would you like to baptize our child?"

"Why, of course, why not!" answered Doña Sebastiana.

"It's a little boy," said the father.

Well, they headed home. They made the arrangements for baptizing the child. Doña Sebastiana had never had a godchild. The child was baptized. She wanted nothing but the best for her godchild.

"Ha, my godchild's going to be one of the best doctors around. The best in all of the communities. In all of the kingdom."

As the little boy got older, she'd come around to visit him. She was very happy with her godchild. And the little boy was happy as well. At last the little boy got older and finished high school. She then sent him to college so he could study to be a doctor. But he didn't take long in becoming a doctor. She said to him:

"Listen, my dear son. I'm going to grant you a talent. You're going to be the best doctor in all of these communities and throughout the kingdom. I'm only going to ask one thing of you. You're going to cure lots and lots of people. And that's going to be good, but I'm going to tell you something. When you get to a home to treat a patient, if I'm at the head of the bed that means I don't want you to cure him. You tell the people that you can't. You tell them you don't know what's wrong with him."

"Oh, of course, my godmother. I'll do whatever you tell me."

She took off and the boy launched his career. He was a very good doctor. He was called from everywhere. He treated people for a long time.

One time there was a king in this kingdom, and his vassals, the king's workmen, came to where the doctor lived. The king was ill and they wanted the doctor to go cure him of his illness. They promised him lots and lots of money, more than what he was earning. Very well, he went with them. When they got to the kingdom, the king's room was very well decorated. The first thing the doctor saw was his godmother. "My," he said to himself, "this is going to be tough."

Nothing doing, he looked at the king and he said to the vassals:

"I don't believe I can do anything for the king because he's already very ill. There's no hope, he's not going to get well."

"Why, I'll pay you and give you so much of my land. I'll pay you lots of money," said the king.

"Oh, my!" said the doctor to himself. "What am I going to do?"

Finally he said to them:

"Yes. Bring me a winch. Put it here, and the rope over there."

The doctor came and lifted the bed and turned it around. As a result Doña Sebastiana ended up at the foot of the bed. The doctor treated the king in a jiffy. That's it, he got well. The doctor went home, very happy and with lots of money. He treated lots more people.

When he was already up in years, he was summoned to another kingdom. This kingdom was very far away. The king was also very, very sick. When the doctor got there, the same thing happened. No sooner had he entered the room and there at the head of the bed was his godmother. She nodded to him not to treat the king. And he—the doctor—said to himself, "Aha." Nothing doing. In a jiffy he told those present what to do, and the doctor once again turned the bed around. He left the kingdom with a lot of money. He continued treating people.

Finally one day his godmother came by. She came to see him.

"Oh, my godmother. How are you?"

"Well, my dear son, and you?"

"Oh, my godmother. I've been very busy."

"Ah, from the look of things I can see, my dear son, that you have been very busy. Let's take a walk. Come with me because I want to chat with you, my dear son."

"Yes, of course, my godmother. Fine, let's go."

Then she took him to this place. They went inside this house. The floor was all covered with candles. Some were large, some very small, but they were all lit. He says to her:

"Oh, my godmother! What's this?"

"My dear son, this is all the people who live on this earth."

"Oh!" said he. "Some are tall, while others are short."

"Yes. The tall ones represent the babies who were born recently. The other candles represent those people who are getting older."

Then he turned to where this small one was and said:

"And this one, godmother, what is it?"

"That one is you," and out goes the candle and the doctor drops dead. And that's it!

■ The King and the Princess

"Well, I don't understand why the princess doesn't laugh. Perhaps she's ill," said the king.

She wouldn't laugh or anything. Why, they even took her to all kinds of doctors, and nothing. No, there wasn't anything wrong with her. She just couldn't laugh, that's all there was to it.

Then the king went and put an announcement in the newspaper saying that the boy who could make the princess laugh, he (the king) would grant him her hand in marriage. He would bequeath him half of his kingdom. Well, many, many boys came and went. But no one made her laugh. They would tell her all kinds of jokes and who knows what all.

Finally, there was this very simpleminded boy. He heard that they were giving the princess away, provided someone made her laugh. He said to his mother:

"Well, I'm going to go."

His mother says to him:

"No. What will you be able to do? Look at how many have come, and they haven't made her laugh."

Well, he showed up, and the princess was sitting down. The maids were serving refreshments. They were serving tea. And they asked the boy:

"Do you want a glass of tea?"

"Why, yes!" said he.

He was sitting at a table, and the princess was at the other end. Then the maid came by again to see if he wanted more tea, and he said to her:

"Yes, I'd like some more."

Finally, the princess stood up and asked him if he wanted more tea.

"Ah, yes! The more tea I drink, the more tea I want" (play on words: "The more I drink of you, the more I love you"), and I understand the princess broke out laughing.

"Goodness gracious!" said the king. "Who has made my daughter laugh?"

"He (the simpleminded boy) made her laugh," said one of the maids.

"Well, I'm going to grant him her hand in marriage so he can marry her."

He married the princess and inherited part of the kingdom.

Juan Manuel Olivas
San Pablo, CO

■ The Catholic and the Jew

This Catholic and a Jew were working in a desert. The Catholic was working for the railroad. The Jew worked for the oil wells. From time to time they ran into each other and challenged one another as to who had the best job. The Jew would say, "Well, we earn this salary and then they pay us. We have certain protections (benefits)." The railroader would then say that they had almost the same protections. Comparing one by one, they came out more or less the same.

But one time the Jew went to town and bought himself a little new truck and stopped by where the Catholic was and said to him:

"Look at what I did. All of this because I have a good job, and so I bought myself a brand-new little truck."

Very well. About a week or so later, the Catholic also went to town and bought himself a new automobile. When he returned, he said to the Jew:

"Look here. I also bought a new automobile, being that I work for the railroad. Let's go for a ride."

They took off. It was about thirty miles to town. That's where they went. When they got there, the Catholic said to the Jew:

"I've got to get back. I have to go see the priest," and so they left.

Then the priest came out and said to the Catholic:

"I'm very glad that you bought a new vehicle. I'm going to bless it," and so he fetched some holy water.

All the Jew could do was to look at him, because he didn't know what all that was about. When the Catholic returned to the railroad, the Jew quietly went back to the oil wells where he worked. The Jew kept thinking and thinking. A while later he went and knocked at the

Catholic's door. The Jew was carrying a hacksaw and a small piece of tailpipe. Then he said to the Catholic:

"Look, you thought you knew more than me."

"Why, no," said the Catholic, "not at all. Why?"

"You took your vehicle to be blessed by the priest. Well, take a look at what I did with mine. I had it circumcised!"

■ A Drunkard

I don't know what sermon the priest was preaching, when all of a sudden he said to everyone:

"If you don't do these things, you're going to go to hell. You're going to be condemned." Then he added:

"Those of you who don't want to be damned, sit down."

And there was a drunkard in Mass who didn't do what the priest said. Everyone sat down. Then the drunkard said to the priest:

"Listen! I believe you and I are the only ones who are going to be condemned," he said, "because everyone else has sat down."

Julia B. Olivas
Pueblo, CO

◼ We're Going to Find You a Wife

A joke that my husband told me is about the married couple who had a son. Now, the son was already quite old—he was about thirty or thirty-two years of age. And there came a time when they told him:

"Tomorrow we're going to town and we're going to find you a wife, because it's high time you got married. We're already quite old. Should we die one of these days, you're going to be left alone."

Next day they hitched up the team of horses to the wagon, climbed on it, and told the son that they were going to find him a girl thirty years old. Very well, off went the horses. Suddenly the boy took off running after them and hollered:

"Wait! Wait just a minute! If you can't find me one thirty year old, bring me back two fifteen year olds."

◼ I'm Left Without Daughters

There was this woman, and she had two daughters who worked far away from where she lived. They would come visit her on the train and return to where they lived on the train. And when the daughters were about to leave, the mother would say:

"Oh! This train takes off with my daughters crying, and as for me, it leaves me here without my daughters (a play on words, *sin ver hijas*, without my daughters, vs. *sin verijas*, without a pubic region)."

Antonia A. Ortiz
El Pueblo, NM

■ A Mischievous Little Old Man

What used to happen a long time ago is that the woman and the man—and it's always been true—didn't agree with one another, you see? That's where all the trouble started.

Long ago the parents presumably talked a bride and groom into getting married. A little old man was summoned. The little old man was very mischievous. He brought a small rope; it was very well braided. It wasn't shredded or anything. He went and lassoed the groom and said to him:

"Come here! Stand right here!"

Then he said to the bride:

"And you, stand right over here!"

He roped both of them. Then he said to the groom:

"Now walk!"

That's what they used to teach you—that wherever the husband went, the wife had to follow. It was a curious thing don't you think?

■ Why I Don't Even Know Him!

Mom used to say that when they went to ask for her hand in marriage so that she could marry Dad, she said to her father:

"But how do you expect me to marry that guy? Why, I don't even know him!"

He said to her:

"But I do!"

Félix Pino
Santa Fe, NM

■ The Priest and the Eggs

This is the story about a priest. He used to come to celebrate Mass in this small village, and he would eat at the home of Celestino's mother. One day when the priest came to celebrate Mass, Celestino's mother forgot to ask him how he wanted his eggs fixed, with or without chile. A short while later Celestino came in and his mother says to him:

"Didn't you go to Mass, my son?"

"No," answered Celestino. "It was already late so I didn't go."

"Do you know that I'm going to feed the priest at noon, but I forgot to ask him whether he wants his eggs with or without chile."

"Mom, I'll go ask him," responded Celestino.

"But how are you going to manage that since people are already in Mass?"

"It doesn't matter if they are or not. I'll find a way."

"Fine, do as you wish."

Celestino then headed for church. He entered and saw that the priest was already celebrating Mass. He went and sat right in front, where the priest could see him. When he saw that the priest turned around to face the people to say *"Dominos obispo,"* Celestino interrupted and said:

"Pater, my *mater* wants to know how you would like your eggs, *blancorio* or *chilorio* (without or with chile)?"

And the priest says to him:

"Tell your *mater, blancorio,* because with *chilorio* my *século seculorio* burns."

75

Elizardo R. Romero
Grants/Chacón, NM

■ The Biggest Lie

Once upon a time these two men used to get together to see who could tell the biggest lie. The two were alone and one said to the other:

"Did you know that at the top of that peak there is an ant?"

And the other fellow says to him:

"I can't see it, but I can hear its footsteps!"

■ A Roaring Bull

This man asked his buddies:

"Listen, boys, tell me, a roaring bull passed in between two white walls. Who knows what the roaring bull really was?"

There they were, he had them in suspense for a long time, but he wouldn't tell them what it was. And they didn't know what it was. It was a fart!

■ A Pig

This is a very short story between two men. One of them asks the other:

"What makes more noise than a pig under a fence?"

And the other man kept thinking, but he didn't know what to answer.

"Two pigs!" said the other man.

Alicia Romero-Vidaurre
Llano de San Juan Nepomuceno, NM

■ In a Jiffy

This woman used to say . . . Okay, her husband's name was Juan and he was quite a party-goer. He liked very much to drink. He'd take off on a binge and when he got back home, there he was after her. Beating her up and mistreating her. The poor thing was already up to her ears. She was scared to death because of the way he mistreated her.

Well, one day he got home from partying, and he was trying to catch her to shake her up. He had her going round and round the kitchen table. First they went one way and then another while he reached out trying to grab her as she fled from him.

I understand that the handle for lifting the lids on top of the woodstove, where you put in wood, was in one of them. Long ago there was always fire in the stoves because the women put food on the stove to cook, and it took all day to prepare. Well, she pulled down her sleeve (used it like a potholder) and grabbed the handle to the lid and put it in front of her for protection. Well, the foolish husband, dizzy as he was, stretched his arm out to grab her and instead of catching her, he grabbed the handle to the stove and burned himself!

Well, that was his holy medicine. He never again beat her up. Oh yeah, he continued in his merry old ways of partying. Fact is, he drank himself to death. But he never again beat up on her. She loved to talk about how she had straightened him out. "Yes," she'd say, "I fixed Juan in a jiffy."

■ The Day I Was Born

Mom used to say that on the day I was born, that morning she had gone early to Cuchilla Pela(d)a to irrigate the crops. Dad had property that belonged to the late Alejandrino under contract, and Mom was the one who cultivated them. Dad was working in Wyoming, and Mom was the one who took care of the land. That year they had planted wheat, oats, barley, pinto beans, peas, horse beans, pumpkins, white, yellow, and blue corn, which was used for making blue-corn gruel and mush.

Well, that morning she got lunch ready and took off on foot to irrigate. Those properties were quite a ways from the village where we lived. I believe they were about a mile, perhaps even farther.

Long about noon she started getting labor pains. The pains kept getting stronger and stronger until she couldn't stand them. She left the water running and headed home. She reached the home of the late Delfina to inform her that she was very ill and for her to go get the midwife right away.

Over at the village where we lived, the homes were very close to one another. They were strung out on either side of the village. Everyone knew right away what was going on, so that the women and the comadres immediately got the bed ready and washed mother up. Mother had the habit of taking off her shoes whenever she irrigated so as not to wear them out; she irrigated barefoot. I understand her feet were full of mud. They washed her as best they could and put her to bed.

They brought in chopped wood. They started heating water and prepared lots of rags. By the time the midwife got there, everything was ready. And Mom used to say that she gave birth in no time at all. She hadn't had a difficult labor. I was born right away. The women who were there would kid her by saying, "Good gracious, Matilde, what if you had given birth in the middle of the pumpkin patch and peas?"

Alfredo Roybal
Mora, NM

■ Don Cacahuate and Doña Cebolla

One time there was Don Cacahuate and Doña Cebolla walking down the railroad tracks when suddenly here comes the train. Doña Cebolla says to Don Cacahuate to move because the train is coming. Don Cacahuate ran far away from the tracks until the train went by. When he came back, Doña Cebolla asked him why he went so far from the railroad tracks. Don Cacahuate said that he did it to be on the safe side, in case the train was moving sideways.

■ The Bad Note

There were these three brothers—a banker, a musician, and one brother who had a speech impediment and lived on a small ranch. A gentleman says to them:

"Explain to me what a bad note is?"

The banker says to him:

"A bad note is when a person goes to the bank and takes out a loan, signs a note (i.e., promissory note) for the money, but fails to pay back the loan. That's a bad note."

Says the musician:

"Whenever the band is playing and one of the musicians strikes the wrong note, that's a bad note."

Then the brother who stammers says to the gentleman:

"A bad note is when a sow gives birth to a bunch of piglets. That's a big pig (*malanota* vs. *marranota*; since he can't pronounce the latter, *marranota*, a huge sow, comes out as *malanota*, a "bad or sour note").

Philomeno Sánchez
San Luis, CO

■ The Brooding Duck

On Sunday my compadre Pánfilo and my comadre Sindicha went to the flea market and bought a couple of ducks—a male and female. Since they weren't able to keep them in the city for very long, they took them to their parents who lived on a small ranch.

With time and a little luck, the female duck turned broody close to the river, and she wouldn't let anyone come near her. One day Doña Perrimplina's comadre Hizquepula went to visit her, and as they chatted, the question of the female duck having turned broody came up. Says Doña Hizquepula:

"Do you know, comadre, that I don't know what the eggs of a female duck look like?"

Doña Perrimplina says to her:

"Let's go. I'll show them to you. The only thing is that this duck is so mean now that it's brooding, that she won't let us come close. But wait. There comes your compadre Pite. Let me give him a holler so he can come help us."

The comadres leave the house, and Doña Perrimplina hollered at him:

"Listen, Don Pite! Come lift the female duck (*pata*) because my comadre Hizquepula wants to see her eggs" (literally, "come lift your leg (*pata*) because my comadre Hizquepula wants to see your balls," a play on words—*huevos*, eggs vs. *huevos*, balls).

This Goat Is Very Shy

A few days after I got home, I was informed that my father was suffering from stomach ulcers. As a remedy (cure) he was told to drink goat's milk before breakfast.

My father started buying milk at the store, but in due time he thought that it would be cheaper buying the goat instead of the milk.

He bought the goat and started milking her. One morning when I happened to get up early, I went to the horse shed where he was milking the goat. The first thing I noticed was that he had one of its legs tied with a rope (probably to a post).

I asked him:

"Is this the new way nowadays of milking a goat—by tying one of its legs?"

He said to me:

"No, my son. The reason I tie one of its legs is because this goat is very shy."

"But what are you talking about?" I said to him. "I've never in my life heard of a goat being shy."

"Well, this one's shy," he said to me. "No sooner I'm going to milk it, and she starts kicking. She won't let me grab her tits!"

Knowing They Belong to Someone Else

Since we had so many friends we soon went into politics. Since we were politicians we were always attending conventions. Following the first convention that we attended at the state capital, we went out for a stroll after supper. No sooner had we walked half a block and we saw two girls coming, about as beautiful as Mona Lisa. I say to Elsie:

"Just look at those chicks, what beautiful slender legs. They can't all be lies for they must drink blue-corn gruel and eat pinto beans. And just look at those headlights, what you call lemons. To me they're more like cabbages . . ."

Elsie says to me:

"Oh, my Little Phil O'Meno! Why do you worry and tarry so very much knowing that when you're not alone the bone to chew on belongs to someone else? I hope you don't bite or smite yourself or they hang you by a chain on a moving train for wanting to have your hands full of the subjects' two objects you're now glaring at and suffering inside by your little lonesome and I beside you. I hope you understand. But never worry or carry on about the brooding chicks, worry about the ones that are laying eggs!"

■ I'm the One Who Takes Care of Them

During the Depression, times for my compadre Campeche and my comadre Nicanora got about as tight as barbed-wire fence. My compadre used to sew sacks (*coser*) not with fire (*cocer*) but with a needle at a factory. But during that year they invented a machine that sewed twenty times faster than he, and that is why they laid him off.

For one whole year he received unemployment and food stamps. Then he had to start stealing to make ends meet because he had three sons: Lito, Tito, and Benito. Later on he would steal because it was necessary, according to him. In the end he was stealing because of stupidity. As the old saying goes, "You can go to the well once too often until you finally end up committing a sin." That's what happened to my compadre Campeche. He was caught stealing, and he was sent to the penitentiary for twenty years.

Soon thereafter my comadre Nicanora applied for public assistance for the children. At the end of two years a representative from the Welfare Department went to see her about her application. When he came to the number of children, the representative said to my comadre Nicanora:

"It says here on the application that you have five children. When Don Campeche went to prison, you only had three. How can that be?"

"Yes, that's true," said my comadre Nicanora, "but you must realize that he's the one in prison, not me. And that's not all, he's not the one supporting them. I'm the one who takes care of them."

■ The Doctor Told Me to Stop Smoking

When I was in the hospital, the doctor told me to stop smoking. One day I was walking down the street smoking a great big cigarette when Chalito Mondragón ran into me and said:

"What in the world is wrong with you, Mister Sánchez? Didn't you almost die from a heart attack? Didn't the doctor tell you to stop smoking?"

"Yes, he did tell me to stop smoking," I said. "For four months I didn't smoke, but when I got well I started all over again with this damn habit and I can't quit."

"If you wish to quit, I'll propose a cure (remedy) for you, and I'll guarantee you that you'll quit smoking within two days."

"Let me have the remedy," I responded. "I can't possibly die from just one remedy. And if by chance I should die from that remedy, once dead there's no remedy (there's nothing we can do about it). A remedy for something that has no remedy (solution) isn't a good remedy."

"This is the remedy," said Chalito. "In the morning for breakfast eat four fried eggs. At noon, you double them. Eat eight fried eggs. For supper, you double that. Eat sixteen fried eggs. Next day for breakfast, you double those. Eat thirty-two eggs."

"Oh, but what in the devil am I going to do with so many fried eggs?" I said to him.

"That's the secret to my remedy," said Chalito to me. "In order to quit smoking, you need lots of eggs (you need a lot of balls)!"

■ My Career as Orator Came to an End

When I was six years old, I started at a saint's school in San Pedro. The saint who supposedly has the keys to heaven.

I could have been a King Solomon for speaking in public, because I started at a very young age. I used to like the poetry that the teacher taught us. I've never been one to be shy and I always liked to get up in front of class to recite poetry. My favorite, the one I liked most, was "Mary Had a Little Lamb."

One day the teacher, Mrs. Andrea Medina, wanted to teach us the most appropriate manner of speaking in public. Since I was the most devilish, she looked at me and says to me:

"Sánchez, stand in front of the class and recite some poetry."

As I said, I wasn't the least bit shy, and since I didn't know her, I stood stiff as a telephone pole, and I began with my favorite poetry.

"Mary had a little lamb."

"No, no, no, no!" she said to me. "Not that way. When one speaks in public, you have to express your actions this way. You have to use your hands. 'Mary had a little lamb,' so put your hands in front. When you say the next line, you put your hands in back like this. *¿Comprende?*"

"Yes, Mrs. Medina, I *comprende*," I said to her.

I coughed a little, cleared my throat, and with a cunning and clear voice, I started reciting:

"Mary had a little lamb in front. Its fleece was white as snow behind. And everywhere that Mary went in front, the lamb was sure to follow her behind."

I don't know what the reason was, but the whole class started laughing. I didn't give a hoot, but when I saw that even the teacher was laughing at me, I said to myself, "This is the last time I'll ever stand in front of a class. Never in my lifetime will I ever make an ass of myself."

That day in San Pedro my career as a public orator, or at least my desire, came to an end.

Eduardo Valdez
Guadalupe (Ojo del Padre), NM

■ The King's Little Tin Can

This is a story about a king, and this king had an only daughter. And a little old lady had an only son and she was very poor. The boy whenever he went to the post office—they lived on a ranch—always liked to buy the newspaper because he liked to read it. And this king one day thought of marrying off his daughter, but he couldn't decide to whom.

Then he said to himself: "This is what I'm going to do. I'm going to hang a little tin can from the beams in this room, and I'm going to put shit in it and a little black cricket. Then I'm going to put an announcement in the newspaper that he who comes and guesses what it is I have in that little can, that one will marry my daughter. If he doesn't guess, he'll pay with his life." You see?

Then the king put an announcement in the newspaper that he who came and guessed what was hanging in that little tin can would marry his daughter. Then this boy, the little old lady's son, got the paper and read the announcement. When he got home, he told his mother that he had found the announcement in the paper, which the king had published, stating that he who guessed what he had inside the little tin can hanging from the beams would marry his daughter. Then the boy told the little old lady that he wanted to go see if he could guess what the king had in the little tin can. The little old lady was reluctant, because whoever didn't guess, well, the king would kill him. You see?

Then the little old lady said to him:

"Well, do you want the king to kill you?"

"Well no," he said to her. "But I want to go see if I can guess, to see if I can marry the king's daughter."

The little old lady was never able to convince him not to go. She finally decided to give him permission to go. And she said to him:

"Get out of here, my little black cricket, you shit-guesser, let the king kill you!"

The boy, still quite enthusiastic, went off to see if he could guess what was in the little can. So, when he arrived at the king's palace, there were quite a few ahead of him, you see, who were taking a chance to see if they could guess, and no one was able to guess. The king was killing all of them; he was taking them out and killing them. Well, finally, it was time for the boy, it was his turn, as we say. They called him. And so the king asked him what the reason was for his visit. So he said to him:

"I saw the announcement you put in the paper, your Majesty, that he who came and guessed what you have hanging in that little tin can would marry your daughter. And if he didn't guess, well, he would pay with his life. And so I came to find out whether I would live or die." This is what the boy told him.

"Well, hurry up!" he said to him. "Stand over here!"

So he stood there and the king told him:

"Let's see! See if you can guess what's in that little tin can. And if you guess, you're going to be my son-in-law."

Then the boy remembered what the little old lady had told him, and so he started to cry. And he said:

"God have mercy on me! Damn me for ever having come here! My mother was right: 'Little black cricket, you shit-guesser.'"

"You got it!" said the king. "That's what it is!"

■ Two Aspiring Young Astronomers

This is an incident involving two young men who were studying to become astronomers. One day they left the city to go out into the countryside. They wanted to observe the heavenly bodies and study the stars, and so they came upon this little old lady who lived alone on a ranch. This little old lady was very poor. All she had was a small room, and in front of it she had a small corral where she kept a donkey. This donkey, whenever it was going to rain, would frolic about and get very happy. The little old lady herself already knew that it was going to rain.

The young men asked her for lodging, and the little old lady says to them:

"Young men, the only thing I have is this small room and just one bed."

She told them that it was going to rain that night. Just the same, the young men told her that they had their own bedding and food and that they would sleep outside because they wanted to study the heavenly bodies, since they were aspiring to become astronomers. The little old lady says to them:

"Very well. When the rain comes, come inside so you won't get wet."

The young men said to each other:

"How does this lady know that it's going to rain?"

"You ask her to tell you how she knows that it's going to rain when there aren't even any clouds," said one of them.

Then the other young man asked her:

"Ma'am, how do you know that it's going to rain tonight?"

The little old lady responded:

"Do you see that donkey that's in the little corral? Whenever he's happy and frisks and jumps about, for sure the rain's coming. There's no ifs, ands, or buts about it."

Shortly after it got dark, clouds began to appear. A short while later it started to rain, and the young men brought their bedding into the small room; it rained all night long. In the morning one of them shakes his pal and says to him:

"Get up! Let's go before it's daybreak. It's embarrassing that a jackass knows more than us."

And so they took off, and the little old lady stayed in bed sleeping.

Floyd E. Vásquez
Chacón, NM

■ The Bedpan

Okay, one time there was this married couple, and it was time for the husband to get home from work. He entered halfway inside the house. The wife was sitting down and she said to him:

"Listen, since you're standing up, stir the potatoes."

He went and stirred the potatoes. Then she said to him:

"Listen, since you're standing up, bring me the tortillas."

He went and brought her the tortillas.

"Listen, since you're standing up, bring me the coffee."

He brought the coffee. The final blow was when she said to him:

"Since you're standing up, bring me the sugar."

And he said to himself: "This mean woman (for taking advantage of him). I can't stand this anymore," and so he got down on his knees. There he was on his knees, and the wife saw him but didn't say anything. He stayed that way the rest of the day—on his knees. He walked everywhere on his knees. Much later when they were going to bed, she said to him:

"Hey, listen, since you're on your knees, fetch the bedpan (i.e., take it out from under the bed)!"

■ A Priest

The archbishop came to check up on the priest. The priest was at a loss as to what to say whenever the archbishop, the most important man, came to see him. Well, the priest went and invited the minister, and so all three went hunting in the mountains. As the night went on, the archbishop says to the priest:

"Woe is me! I don't know what to say, except that I'm having a nicotine fit. Oh, this smoking. Father, this smoking habit of mine."

"Smoking? Think nothing of it. Smoke all you want."

A few seconds later, the priest then says:

"Not me. My bad habit is alcohol. I like whiskey very much. Lots! But tequila is what I like for getting drunk."

"Oh, well, here we are among friends. Drink as much as you like."

Then they both looked at the minister, and he didn't say anything.

"Well, what's with you?" said the archbishop.

"Oh, not me," answered the minister. "What I like is to gossip."

Cruzita Vigil
Corazón, NM

■ The Little Old Lady and the Little Old Man

Oh, I do have this joke about the rooster! Okay. I understand there were two old-timers, a little old lady and a little old man. And they had chickens. One morning the little old man said to the little old lady,

"That rooster is no longer worth its salt. It's too old. It no longer cuts it with the chickens. I'm going to see if I can find a young one."

He went and brought back a new rooster, and as soon as the new one saw the old one, he went after him. No sooner he saw this and the little old man went in the house in a very big hurry.

"Give me the rifle that's over there!"

"Well, what are you going to do?" said the little old lady.

"I'm going to kill that rooster. Instead of getting a cock, I got one that's queer."

■ Saint Peter Was God's Companion

Saint Peter was God's companion, and still is. But when God took leave of Saint Peter, the day when He went to heaven, Saint Peter followed Him nonetheless. God opened the door slightly and said to Saint Peter:

"What are you doing here, Saint Peter?"

"Nothing. I came to see you. I don't want to separate myself from You."

And he began inching in, little by little. Saint Peter kept inching in, little by little, until he was way inside heaven without God letting him in. When he was well inside, God said to him:

"You have made your way in, Saint Peter, but you will turn into a rock."

Saint Peter then replied:

"Yes, but with eyes."

¡ Chistes !

EL humor hispano

Manuel B. Alcón
Ocaté/Mora, NM

▨ Un chamaquito muy avanzado

Este chamaquito siempre andaba preguntando preguntas por información. En veces iba a visitar a su tía María a quien no le gustaba muncho limpiar la casa. Un día jue a verla y cuando volvió de su paseo le preguntó a su mamá que si era verdá que vinimos de tierra o polvo.

Su mamá le dijo que sí. Luego le preguntó que si vamos a volver a polvo, y su mamá le respondió que sí.

—Tierra semos y tierra volveremos.

—¿Pues sabe usté que debajo de la cama de mi tía María hay alguien?

—¿De veras?—contestó la mamá.

—Y además que la persona que viene o va deber ser una persona muy grande—dijo el chamaquito.

—¿Qué te hace dicir eso?—preguntó la mamá.

—¡Por la pila de tierra que hay bajo la cama de mi tía!

▨ Los cientistas sábenlotodo

Este par de educaos profesores después de haber echao a Dios de las escuelas y de las ofecinas públicas, decidieron que ya podían competir con el Señor. Confrontaron a San Pedro en las *Pearly Gates*.

—¿Qué hacen aquí?—preguntó San Pedro.

—Queremos hablar con Dios—dijo uno d'ellos.

—Espérensen un momento—dijo San Pedro.

Luego se puso en el *Internet* y le mandó un *e-mail* a Dios. Pronto respondió Dios, y les dijo, sabiendo qué traiban entre unas estos profesores.

—¿Qué es su problema? Ya saben que no están en muy buen término conmigo.

—Pues vinimos a decirle que ya no lo necesitamos—dijo uno de los cientistas—. Ya podemos hacer too lo que se necesita hacer y posible mejor que Usté. Ya juimos a la luna, inventamos el poder atómico, y ahora hemos hecho munchos clones, en animales y ahora en la gente.

—Muy bien—dijo Dios—. Pero su palabra de ustedes no me satisface ni apenas. A ver si me dan prueba.

—¿Qué prueba necesita—preguntó uno d'ellos.

—Que me hagan un hombre de tierra—les dijo Dios.

—¡Kids' stuff!—dijo el más avanzao de los cientistas.

Salieron pa juera y les dijo Dios,

—¿A ver qué tal?

Uno d'ellos comenzó hacer una pila de tierra. Luego les dijo Dios,

—¡Párenle ahi! Ésta es mi tierra. Hagan su propia tierra.

Una rana

Toos los animalitos de la selva se juntaron y tenían clase. Vino el profesor, que era un león. El león les dijo,

—Hoy vamos a entretenernos en el río. Vamos a tener munchos chistes.

—¡A qué güeno!—dijo la rana—. ¡Qué bonito!

—Y luego después vamos a la tienda y les voy a dar un *treat*—dijo el león.

—¡A qué güeno—dijo la rana.

Ahi siguió. Cada vez que dicía el professor algo, dicía la rana, "¡A qué güeno!"

Al último se cansó el profesor de prometeles tanto y dijo,

—A ese bocón, a ése no lo vamos a llevar.

Luego dice la rana,

—¡Ya fregaron al crocodilo!

Tres personas

Había estas tres personas que iban juntas toos los traques. Uno era un nuevo mexicano. Otro era un californiano. Y l'otro era un tejano. Ahi iban caminando cuando se les hizo noche. Too oscuro. Estáa poco malo el tiempo. Parecía que iba llover. Siguieron caminando y llegaron a un rancho. Tocaron la puerta y salió un ranchero y les dijo,

—¿Qué pasa?

—Hemos caminao too el día—dijo uno de ellos—. Andamos muy cansaos y no tenemos dónde quedarnos. *So*, si nos pudiera dar onde quedarnos esta noche …

Ya les dijo el viejito, el ranchero,

—Seguro. Nada más que no tengo más que un catre y no caben más de dos de ustedes. Loo tengo un trochil. Tengo un marranito. Si quieren pasar la noche aquí con nosotros, están bien venidos. Y dijieron los tres,

—Sí, vale más algo que nada.

—Bueno—dijo el ranchero—. Pues vamos a dividir la noche tal tiempo porque cada uno vaya al trochil y los otros dos al sofacito—al catre.

Bueno, pues, hicieron el cambalache y primero le tocó al nuevo mexicano. Jue el nuevo mexicano al trochil. Dos minutos ya estaba patrás, y dijo,

—No. No puedo aguantale más a ese marrano. Ora tú.

Jue antonces el californiano. Entró el californiano allí con el marranito. Como tres o cuatro minutos aquí lo tienes patrás. Luego le tocaba al tejano, y entró éste onde estaba el marranito. Allá se estuvo. Vieron los otros dos el reló tres minutos cuando oyeron la puerta sonar. Parecía que la querían quebrar. Abrieron la puerta y entró el marranito tapándose las narices, y dijo,

—Yo no sé, pero ese tejano, si juera marrano ni nosotros lo aguantáranos.

Un tiburón

Iban tres amigos en un barquito: un mexicano, un italiano, y un francés. Pues ahi iban y se hundiaron. Se hundió el barquito y comezaron a nadar. Vino un tiburón y pescó al mexicano y se lo comió. Luego pescó al italiano. Se lo comió tamién, pero al francés lo dejó ir. Luego le dijo otro tiburón,

—¿Por qué no te comites al francés?

—No—le dijo—. Pus, l'último francés que yo comí toavía me arde la trasera.

Este muchito malcriao

Ahi estaba este muchito malcriao pataleando las piernas. Yo creo que renegando tamién. Llegó el padre, y le dijo el muchito,

—¡Oiga padre! ¿Usté dice mentiras?

Y le dice el padre,

—No. No me permiten dicir mentiras a mí.

—Oh, ¿y qué sabe muncho de religión?

—Sí, sí, pus soy padre. Yo estudié pa eso.

—Pues, ¿dónde está Dios?

—Dios está dondequiera.

—¿Y está en casa?

—Sí, sí, está en tu casa.

—¿Y en el camino?

—Sí, está en el camino.

—¿En el corral de mi tío?

—Tamién en el corral de tu tío está.

—Pa que veiga que sí miente—le dice el muchito—. ¡Porque mi tío ni corral tiene!

Un indio

Este indio quería hacerse cristiano y lo llevaron al catacismo. Le estuvieron indoctrinando. Ya cuando se les hizo a los padres que estaba listo pa 'cer la Primera Comunión, lo trujo uno de los padres adelante del arzobispo. Éste le preguntó los rezos y los supo muy bien y todo. Luego le dice,

—¿Sabes el cre(d)o?—y les dijo el indio que sí y se lo rezó al arzobispo.

—¿Crees tú en Dios?

—Sí, sí creo.

—¿Y crees tú que Dios va a juzgar a los vivos y a los muertos?

—Seguro que sí creo—le dijo—. ¡Pero ahi verá que no viene!

En su patarrabo

Este chiste es diún indio que andaba ahi en su patarrabo. Viene un mexicano y le dice,

—Oye, indio, ¿cómo es que no te vistes? Ahi andas con el rabo de fuera. ¿Qué no te da frío?

Y le dice el indio,

—No. ¡Nalga mía con cara tuya!

Virginia Alfonso
Pueblo, CO

▪ Sarcasmo de una pareja

Marido:	¿Dónde está mi deodorizante para oler yo bonito y complacerles a las chicas?
Esposa:	¿Cuál querido? ¿El de bolita?
Marido:	No, el de sobaco.
Esposa:	Ni siquiera me dites los días.
Marido:	Pues, buenos días.
Esposa:	Los días son de Dios y no del diablo. Luego ya inmediatamente cuando se dan los días, se habla con política y se dice, "Buenos días te dé Dios."
Marido:	Ya estoy de acuerdo. Comenzaré de nuevo. Buenos días te dé Dios. ¿Cómo amanecites?
Esposa:	Acostada. ¿Qué creyes que duermo parada?
Marido:	¿Qué pasa? Hablas como si hubieras comido carne de perro.
Esposa:	¿Por qué querido? ¿Qué te falta un pedazo?
Marido:	Sabes que tienes tus modos como tienes tu cara.
Esposa:	¡Ay naretón! Hace tiempo que deseo preguntarte. ¿Qué si ésa es tu nariz propia o te estás comiendo un plátano?
Marido:	Oh, bésame el sonfiate.
Esposa:	Chatito. Lo hiciera pero, ¿qué se te olvidó que es parte de lo que te falta porque te lo remudaron para remendarte la cara?
Marido:	¡Ladra perro nomás no muerdas!
Esposa:	¡Vete al infierno!
Marido:	De allá vengo, pero no estabas en casa.
Esposa:	Bien me lo decía papá que no me casara.

Marido:	Bien me lo decía el mío, que cuando fuera a descoger un perrito que mirara que la perra no fuera cuerera.
Esposa:	¿Pues qué pasó? ¿Por qué él mismo su consejo no lo aplicó?
Marido:	Jamás te rogaré aunque me pegue piojo y me muera de tristeza.
Esposa:	Pues vete apreviniendo para morir enjertado.
Marido:	¿Quién iba a pensarlo que esto es a lo que yo iba a llegar? ¡A mí tanto que me gustaban tus besos!
Esposa:	Sí, pero desde que te resurates el bigote saben lo mismo que a un huevo sin sal.
Marido:	¡Vieja maldita! Cuando te conocí te veías tan mansita.
Esposa:	Los burros son burros y tanto le pican la cruz que al fin reparan.
Marido:	¿Quieres más?
Esposa:	Me sigues con esas chifletas me vas a perder.
Marido:	Más se perdió en el diluvio y nada era mío.
Esposa:	Bueno. ¡Para que más reproches! Ya que nos casamos nos fregamos. ¿Qué se te antoja para el desayuno? ¡El cielo es límite!

Jesusita Aragón
Las Vegas, NM

Las once cabras

Una vez le preguntó un maestro a un muchacho que parecía poco tonto, que si había un hatajo de once cabras en un corral y se salía una, ¿cuántas cabras se quedaban?

Y les dijo el muchacho,

—¡Ni una!

Es porque las cabras que están atrás, siempre siguen a la otra que va delante. ¡Asina son las cabras!

Un cerro de arena

Éste era un profesor en el colegio, y estaban munchos estudiantes, y estaba un pobre que siempre lo tenían olvidao, como es costumbre. Siempre hay uno. Muy quieto el muchacho este. Es que dijo el profesor, "Voy a ver qué saben éstos." Y les dijo,

—Muchachos. Escuchen. Les voy hacer una pregunta. Allá muy lejos está un cerro de arena. ¿Cuántos sacos necesitan pa 'char esa arena?

Unos dijieron que diez; otros cien, y asina. Logo dijo, "Voy a ver aquél, el calladito," y jue.

—¿Y tú qué dices? ¿Qué dices tú? ¿Cuántos sacos necesitan pa 'char la arena?

Y le dice el calladito,

—Pus yo le diré una cosa. Si el saco es del tamaño del cerro, nomás uno necesitan.

Mi compadre Jesús

Una vez jueron a visitalo sus cuñadas a mi compadre Jesús. Estaba en el hospital aá en Colorao. Aá vivían él y su esposa. Jueron sus cuñadas a velo, y le dice una de ellas, porque él traiba uno d'esos camisones del hospital, le dice,
    Señora Santana,
    Señor San José,
    abaje la pata,
    se le ve no sé qué.
Y le respondió él,
    Señora Santana,
    Señor San José,
    déjelo que se mire,
    al cabo que no es
    pa usté.

Una hoja de maiz

Aquí en Las Vegas pasó esto, lo que le voy a contar. Este hombre era muy amigo de un juez, de don Luis Armijo. Y era malo don Luis, muy bravo, pero era muy amigo de la gente d'este hombre, y el pobre, ranchero él, no sabía que responder en la corte. No sé por qué lo pondrían en la corte.

—Ven acá, Segundo—así se llamaba, Segundo Baca—. Mira. Si un ranchero fuma una hoja de maiz, ¿cuántas lambidas necesita pa pegar ese cigarro?

—Oiga amigo don Luis. Si es tan baboso como usté, nomás una lambida necesita. Con una lambida le sobra.

Johnnie Archibeque
Bernalillo, NM

▦ Las vacas

Esta señora y otras trabajaban con el sacerdote. Un día él ordenó que cada familia donara un animal, por lo menos una vaca. Cuando vino la señora a la casa, le dice a su marido que tiene que donar la vaca, cual nomás una tenían pa la leche. El marido le dijo que no, pero al fin tanto le rogó la mujer que dijo que lo haría. Pues juntó buen hatajo de vacas ella pal sacerdote.

Luego vido un pastor el marido pa que cuidara las vacas. Un día de verano se durmió el pastor abajo de un árbol, y se fueron todas la vacas, como las vacas conocen su corral. Pues hacía tiempo que se fueron las vacas. Las siguieron a la vaca del marido pal corral de ende estababa más antes.

La señora le había dicho a su esposo que Dios les iba a rendir cuando la vaca la entregaron. Una mañana el esposo se estaba haciendo la barba y vido que se llenó el corral de vacas. Luego le dice a su señora,

—Bien dijistes tú que nos iba rendir Dios. ¡Mira cuántas vacas están en el corral!

Cuando el pastor supo que estaban en su corral, fue por ellas. El marido no quiso entregarlas. Le dice al pastor,

—¡A poco el padre dice mentiras! Él dijo que Dios nos iba rendir y ésas son las que me rindieron a mí.

Antonces el padre pa arreglar el negocio dijo,

—El que me dé los buenos días primero por la mañana se queda con las vacas.

Pues cerca del portal de la casa del padre estaba un árbol muy coposo. Se fue el marido en la noche y se subió al árbol. En la mañana que el padre salió pa fuera, el marido brincó del árbol y le dice de sorpresa,

—¡Buenos días padre!—y se quedó con todas las vacas.

La mesa es compañera

La mesa es compañera de la silleta, siempre. Un día estaba la silleta 'nojada con la mesa, y la mesa le pregunta que si qué pasaba,

—¿Por qué estás 'nojada conmigo?

La silleta responde y le dice,

—¡A lo menos a ti te pone el plato la cocinera, pero a mí nomás me pone las nalgas!

Mi perro tiene fiebre

El novio convidó a su novia al *show* y a cenar y cuando llegó por ella a su casa, le dice ella,

—Amor mío, no puedo ir contigo porque mi perro tiene fiebre, y tendré que llevarlo al doctor.

Le dice el novio,

—No tienes que hacer esos costos. Ve a la hielera y agarra la mostaza.

—¿Y por qué la mostaza—le dice la novia.

—¡Eso es lo que le pones a un perro caliente!

Andrés Archuleta
Trujillo, NM

▨ Dos viejos sentaos en la resolana

Güeno, pus le voy a dicir una tontera. Había dos viejos sentaos en una resolana, porque ya no podían hacer nada más. Platicando, ¿eh? Y los vieron dos viejas, y dijieron,

—Vamos hacer estos viejos levantar la cabeza.

Pus ya eos estaan muy viejos, como yo. Y se plantaron eas muncho. Se vistieron, se pusieron sombreros y todo, y pasaron por onde estaan los viejos. Levantó uno la cabeza, y dice,

—¡Mira!—le dijo al otro—, que panteras van.

Pero jue too. Y dijieron eas,

—Pero, ¿qué tal? No se levantaron ni nada.

Otro día dijieron eas,

—Pus vamos a ver si los hacemos levantarse.

Se pusieron de éstos, como les digo yo, *picnick*. ¿Cómo les dicen? *Shorts*. Y los viejos se mantenían ahi, pus ya no hacían naa. Y pasaron otra vez eas, y las vido uno.

—¡Mira!—le dijo al lotro—, las piernas, ni plancharon la ropa.

Pus ya eran puras arrugas.

La tortilla

Éste es un cuento de don Cacahuate y de doña Cebolla. Tenían un muchito, ¿eh? Y estaba llorando el muchito por tortilla, ¿sabe? Ya le dijo don Cacahuate,

—¿Qué tiene este muchacho?—le dijo,—qué está llore y llore ahi.

Le dijo ea,

—Está llorando porque le dites la tortilla y está fría.

—¡Oh *shite!*—le dijo él.

La agarró la tortilla y se la metió en el sobaco, ¿ves? Y loo le dice,

—¡Toma!

La agarró el muchito.

—¿Qué pasa?—le dijo el papá.

—Me quemé.

Entró al confesionario

Había unos vecinos, y le había robao, güeno, juzgaba uno d'ellos, casi estaba cierto, que le había robao un vecino su vaca. Su vaca, ¿ve? Y no jallaba cómo sacar la verdá. Loo jue con el padre, con el sacerdote, el de la vaca perdida, y le dijo,

—Padre, estoy casi seguro que aquél me robó mi vaca. ¿Por qué no le confiesa? Hazle una confesión con él, a ver si le saca la verdá.

Pus loo comenzaron ahi todos a trabajale, al que se robó la vaca, que se confesara. Él nunca se confesaba, pero la gente ahi estaba,

—Vale más que se confiese, vale más que, . . .

Al fin lo convinieron, y jue a confesarse. Entró al confesionario. Ya le dijo el padre,

—Pues dice el vecino—le dijo—, que usté le robó la vaca.

No oyó. En esos tiempos habían puesto un confesionario nuevo en la iglesia. Y le volvió a decir el padre,

—Dicen que usté le robó la vaca al campesino.

No oyó. Antonces salió el padre del confesionario y le dijo,

—Oye, te estoy hablando. ¿Qué no oyes?

—No—le dijo él—. No oigo. No se oye nada.

—¿Cómo que no se oye?

—No—le dijo—. Enbócate tú. Verás te tú y te confieso yo.

Se enbocó el padre. Y ya le dijo el de la vaca,

—Toa la gente dice que vives con la conventera.

No respondió el padre. Y aquél le volvió a dicir,

—Dice la gente que vives con la conventera.

No oyó el padre. Y al fin se envoltió y le dijo,

—¿Qué no oítes?

—No—le dijo el padre—. No sirve este confesionario. Voy a dicir que me pongan otro.

Miguel Antonio Arellano
Amalia, NM/Pueblo, CO

¡Éste es tu tacho!

Una vez, en un tiempo, había una gente, indios, que vivía en Farmington. Ahi sembraban de a poquito. Los indios sembraban maiz y es que se daba muy güeno. Pos un indio sembró su maiz y subió muy pronto el elote. Estaba tan güeno que pasaban los gringos por ahi y empezaron a jallar elotes y a robárselos. Ya se la habían jallao de írselos a robar.

Loo jue una gringa a robar, y el indio se jue a la milpa y ya estaba esperándola. Y la gringa aquí juntando elotes y el indio ahi quitándose la ropa. Toca que ya cuando agarró su brazada de elotes pa irse ella, rónpele él de aá en peloto del todo. Ella iba juyendo. Entonces toda la gente era católica. Iba juyendo y que ya la alcanzaba el indio, y es que dijo ella,

—Padre mío San Acacio. Líbrame de este indio.

—¡Aquí está tu tacho!—es que le dijía él a ella—. ¡Éste es tu tacho!

Un pastor

Una vez compré un Model T y salí en él desde Miami, por el estado de Arizona. Tú sabes que el estado de Arizona es puro, puro, es puro desierto. Pos ahi iba enbolao yo. Pa mí no había caminos, no había altos, no había arroyos. Vinía un alto, lo subía y lo bajaba. Pa cuando se metió el sol, estaba yo de vuelta en la Plaza. Y le digo yo a la mujer:

—Mañana voy a California en mi carro. Ahi vuelvo con el sol.

—Oh, no vas.

—Sí voy. ¿Por qué no ha de ir?

—Pero no la haces. El sol camina murre viento.

Otro día llené el carro de gaselín, bien, bien lleno. Nomás aclaró, que salió el sol, le pegué yo pal rumbo de Indio, California. Ahi voy yo por el desierto. Aá no había caminos por el desierto. Cuando ya eran las diez o las once, que ya era el sol de mediodía, ya mi carro se iba apagando con el calor y todo.

Alcancé a ver un pastor andar aá con unas borreguitas. Dije, "Voy a ver qué tan lejos está pa llegar a Indio."

Pues jui pallá. Voy y le digo,

—¡Oye! ¿Qué andas haciendo?

—Cuidando borregas.

Ahi estuve mirando y loo le digo,

—¿Qué tanto me falta a mí pa Indio?

—¡Mire!—me dijo—. ¡Ya nomas las plumas le faltan!

Lucinda Atencio
Bernalillo, NM

San Antonio

Este muchacho vivía con su padre. Ya estaba el muchacho grande, y un día le dijo su padre,

—Corre pídile a San Antonio que te ayude a buscar un trabajo. Güeno. Se jue pa' la iglesia y le rezó las oraciones. Loo jue y le dijo— era el San Antonio grande, y le dijo,

—¡Oye San Antonio! Vale más que me ecuentres un trabajo. Si no, te voy a apuñalar.

Y el padre (el cura) que estaba atrás de San Antonio oyó todo. Güeno. Ya se jue el muchacho, y vino el padre y quitó el San Antonio grande y puso el chiquito. Otro día vino el muchacho y le dijo,

—Oyes, *Junior,* ¿ónde está tu padre?

La garra

Güeno, estaba esta mujer y estaba su hijo. La mamá iba a ver a su esposo allá onde estaba trabajando junto del camposanto. Cerca de la casa ahi había un perrito muy bravo. No más en cuanto salió la mamá y se le cayó la bandana, y le gritó el muchacho, el hijo,

—¡La garra mamá, la garra!

Salió corriendo la mamá a todo vuelo. Cuando llegó al cerco del camposanto le dijo el muchito, que iba corriendo detrás d'ella,

—¿Pus por qué corrió mamá?

¡Pus me dijites que me iba agarrar el perrito!

El zancarrón

Esque esta mujer era una muy traviesa. Cuando se iba su marido pus colgaba el zancarrón ea en la puerta, tú sabes, pa' que supiera el amante que no estaba su marido. Una vez esque se olvidó meter el zancarrón, y llegó el marido del trabajo. Mas al rato pus era un ruidazo en la puerte de la casa. Esque le dijo ea,

—Pus yo no sé. Alguien se murió. Yo creo que vinieron a avisarnos. Son ánimas. Son ánimas.

—Sí—esque le dijo el marido—. Pus rézales. Ya a mí me enfadó ese ruidaso.

—Güeno—le dijo ea.

Ánima que andas penando, de mí alcanzarás el perdón.

Mi marido está en la casa, se me olvidó el zancarrón.

Ea colgaba un zancarrón, ¿ves?, pa' cuando se iba el marido, y olví-dase, y ahi estaba el hombre (el amante). Y ea conque, "Ánima que andas penando, de mí alcanzarás el perdón. Mi marido está en la casa, se me olvidó meter el zancarrón."

'Taba ea dando la oracion tan linda pa' las animas. El viejo (marido) tonto se creyó.

Las sardinas

Este hombre no sabía inglés y le hacía las señas al cajero, detenién-dose la nariz, que quería sardinas. Loo que le dicía el cajero,

—Yo no sabe—hasta que lo agarró el hombre del hombro y le dicía que oliera.

—¡Oh, sardinas! Sí, sí sardinas—, dijo después de olerle los dedos (acabaa de comer sardinas), pero al principio el cajero no sabía qué quería, porque el hombre no sabía dicir sardinas en inglés.

Las dos comadres

Llegó este compadre y tocó la puerta. Ahi estaba tocando la puerta, pero las comadres no hacían caso.

—No abra comadre. No abra.

—Ábrame. Vengo helao, helao—que vinía helao.

—No le abra comadre. Está envolao.

—Comadre, comadre, ábrame. Vengo tieso, tieso.

—Ábrale comadre, isque viene vendiendo queso.

Los pollitos

Este hombre jue y quitó la gallina culeca y se echó él en los huevos. Estaban naciendo los pollitos. Iban naciendo los pollitos uno por uno.

—Ahi viene. Ahi viene—isque dicía él.

Ahi estuvo, ahi estuvo hasta que nacieron todos los pollos. Luego se levantó y vino la gallina y pícale.

—No. Si estos pollos son míos. Yo los saqué. Yo los saqué.

No dejó llegar a la gallina onde estaban los pollitos. Pues al fin él se quedó con los pollos. Se los sacó. Se los llevó. Después ahi andaba platicando que había puesto pollos. Estaba medio, medio.

Un bol di oro

Éste era un indio, y estaban dos ricos. Estaban comiendo en una mesa, y el indio quería comer—tenía hambre—pero no lo llamaban, no lo convidaban. Luego fue pallá él y se paró y les dijo,

—Oigan, señores, ¿cuánto dan por un *bol* di oro?

—¡Arrímate a comer! ¡Arrímate! ¡Come!

Comió el indio. Cuando ya llenó dijo,

—Ya yo vá.

—¿Qués el *bol* di oro?

—Cuando yo jallará, cuando yo jallará.

Elba C. de Baca
Las Vegas, NM

▨ A Saragosa

Un día se encontró un cuervo con su amigo el perico. Le dice el cuervo,

—Buenos días Perico. Yo voy de prisa para Saragosa.

Le respondió Perico,

—Hola Cuervo. Irás para Saragosa, ¡si Dios quiere!

Dice el cuervo,

—¡Yo voy quiera Dios o no quiera!

Pues se fue el cuervo volando, cuando vino un terromote terrible y lo tumbó en un pozo.

El siguiente mes se encontró el cuervo al perico. El perico le dice,

—¿Para dónde vas tan apurado?

—Oh—le dice el cuervo—. ¡Ahi voy para Saragosa o pa el pozo!

▨ Dos Hippies

Un día iban dos *Hippies* por el monte platicando. Le dice uno de ellos,

—¿Sabes lo que pasó? Estaba leyendo que el Santo Papa se cayó en el baño y se quebró una pierna.

Le pregunta el otro *hippie*,

—¿Pues qué es un baño?

Le responde el *hippie*,

—¿Y cómo voy a saber yo? ¡Yo no soy católico!

La luna y el gato

La luna le dice al gatito,

—¡Tan chiquito y con bigotes!

Le responde el gatito,

—¡Y tú que no te da vergüenza mirando toda la noche lo que no te importa!

¿Qué tú también compraste leña?

Un día llegó un leñero a una casa donde estaba solo un perico. Gritó el leñero,

—¿Quieren comprar leña?

Le respondió el perico de adentro de la casa,

—¡Sí, ahi tírela!

Cuando volvió su dueño se enojó mucho con el perico. Esa tarde el dueño empezó a regañar a su hijito por ser malo. El niño se soltó llorando. Le gritó el perico,

—¿Qué tú también compraste leña?

Usted mi señorita escoja

Juan y Justo se fueron para el baile. Al rato llegó una joven llamada Tila, y su amiga. Tila estaba coja. Le dice Juan a Justo,

—Apuesto que no vas para donde está Tila y le dices "coja."

Le respondió Justo,

—¡Y cómo no! Ven conmigo y verás que si le digo "coja."

Pues Juan y Justo se fueron para donde estaba Tila y le ofrece Justo una rosa y le dice,

—De esta flor y de esta rosa, usted mi señorita escoja.

José Ignacio Cantú
Manassa, CO

▨ Los casaos

Si es verdá, para allá va, si es mentira, ya está urdida. Pues se casó (casaron) un hombre y una mujer. Se casaron por el padre. Y usté sabe que el matrimonio por el padre siempre se debe respetar. Por eso ellos estaban respetando. Ellos salieron malos casaos. Y le dijo el hombre a la mujer,

—Pues si no hemos de vivir bien, es mejor apartarnos.

—Bueno—le dice ella—, pero tendremos que ir a ver al padre pa que nos descase.

Se fueron a ver al padre. Llegan allí a onde está el padre y le dicen que se querían descasar, que ya no querían vivir juntos.

—Bueno—les dice el padre—, vengan mañana listos lo mismo que el día que se casaron, bien vestidos para descasarlos.

Pues llegaron allá onde estaba el padre. El padre estaba ya en las gradas, ya revestido pa descasarlos. Y agarró el incensario en la mano y estuvo hablando el padre y amagándoles con el incensario, a uno una vez y al otro otra. Cada vez les pegaba más reciecito. En el último, que ya les estaba pegando, ya les estaba dando golpes con el incensario en la cara y ya empezó a saliles sangre a uno y al otro. Ya le dice la mujer al padre,

—¿Pues qué es lo que va hacer con nosotros?

—A matar uno—le dice el padre.

—Que así no—dice la mujer—, que vale más vivir juntos que no muerto uno de los dos.

—Pues del otro modo no se pueden separar.

Ahi se arrepintieron. Salieron de allí y fueron a vivir bien.

Adrián Chávez
Armijo (Albuquerque), NM

▩ Dos padres

Estaban estos dos padres, y uno de ellos era muy tomador. Tomaba muncho. A veces no sabía ni que andaba tomao, pero de todos modos, siempre iba a ver a su compañero, muy seguido. En una de estas ocasiones dejó de tomar.

Pues una mañana salió a depositar un sobre y no sabía dónde estaba la estafeta. Aá más adelante se encontró un niño. Ya le habla el padre,

—Oye güen niño—le dice—. ¿Y dónde está la estafeta por aquí?

—Pos ai, tantas cuadras pallá.

De repente le dice el padre,

—¿Y por qué no juites a la escuela hoy?

—No, pos por esta y esta razón.

Empezó a aconsejalo el padre,

—Mira hijito—le dice—. Vale más que vayas a la escuela; es muy importante. ¿Eres cristiano?

—Sí y no.

—Vale más que le pongas más sentido—le dice—, porque pa que los güenos niños como tú conozcan el camino pal cielo.

—¡Um jum! Pero usté tanto que ha rezao—le dijo el niño—, y no sabe ni siquiera el camino pa la estafeta.

Filiberto Esquibel
Cañada del Medio, NM

■ El Cholesterol

Te voy a contar un chiste poco simple. Tú sabes como hay algunos que tienen muncho *cholesterol*. Estaba este viejito. Muy pesao. Y le dijo la mujer,

—Apenas alcanzas resuello. Vamos al dotor. Vale más que vayas. Vamos.

Y se lo llevó. Fue y habló con el dotor. Ella hablaba mejor inglés que él. Ella habló con el dotor y le dijo qué quería. El marido se quedó allí esperando. Luego el dotor llamó al viejito, y le dijo,

—Déjeme examinarlo. Es pa su bien suyo.

Sí, estaba muy alto el *cholesterol*. Y le dijo el dotor,

—¿Qué es su almuerzo suyo?

—Yo me sampeyo unos cuatro huevos.

—Uh, ahi está malo—le dijo, y llamó a la esposa—. Óigame señora, este hombre tiene que cortarle los huevos en la mañana.

Al día siguiente en la mañana salió la viejita con el cuchillo.

—¿Qué demonio vas hacer con ese cuchillo?

—Pues esto me encargó el dotor—le respondió ella.

—Dile al dotor como cuesta. A mí no me vas a tocar con ese cuchillo.

■ Gene Autry

Estaban estos dos músicos y le dice uno al otro,

—Sabes qué le pasó a Gene Autry? A Gene Autry lo pescaron los indios, y lo amarron diún pinabete. Empezaron arrimar leña seca. Y vino Gene Autry y le gritó a su caballo, *Champion*.

Salió el caballo hacer su mandao. Salió juyendo el caballo. No se tardó ni media hora. Cayó el caballo reciote cerca de Gene Autry con una mujer en pelota. Muy linda. Muy cuerota. Y Gene Autry le dio un revés al caballo. Le dice,

—*I sent you for a posse, not a pussy!*

Félix Esquivel
San Pablo, CO

El del becerro

Un nuevomejicano fue a California y llegó a una casa en donde estaban dos comiendo y no lo llamaban a comer. Y le dijo uno de ellos,

—¿Qué clas de pais es donde tú vives?

—¡Oh, allá es un pais grande, un pais rico!

—¿Qué riquezas hay?

—Que todas las familias en Nuevo Méjico, cuando toman su comida usan una cucharita pa cada bocadito.

Y aquéllos se almiraban que pa cada bocado había cucharita, pero él no les dijo que la cucharita era la tortilla.

—Pero además de esto—les dijo—, allá las vacas no son como éstas de aquí.

—¿Por qué?

—Porque éstas de aquí paren de a un becerro y aquéllas de allá paren de a dos.

—¿Y cómo hacen pa mantener dos becerros?

—Pues bien, así como ustedes hora. Mientras uno mama, el otro está mirando.

El que se quería casar con su abuela

Un hombre que tenía un hijito como de cuatro años y le dice éste a su papá,

—Papá, y cuando yo sea grande, ¿podré casarme con mi abuela?

—¡Eya, bribón! ¿Y por qué te quieres casar con mi madre?

—¡Toma!—le dice el muchacho—. ¿Cómo usté sí se ha casao con la mía?

El que no convidó a sus padres

Era un joven que pidió mujer y le dieron pa tal fecha y empezó a convidar amigos. Y viendo uno de sus amigos que a sus padres [los del joven] no convidaba, le preguntó que si por qué a sus padres no convidaba para sus fiestas, y, sollozando, le respondió,

—Porque tengo un sentimiento. Cuando ellos se casaron, a mí no me convidaron.

Carmelita Gómez
Aguilar, NM

Mi tío Pedro era mure ronco

Mi agüelita tenía un hermano, y era medio baboso. En ese tiempo andaba de con el Coco. Isque le dijo mi agüelita a su hermano.

—Oyes. ¡Cállate!

—¿Qué?—contestó él.

Era mure ronco. Mi tío Pedro era mure ronco. Pus que le dijo a ella que iba a rezar el Padre Nuestro. Por rezar el Padre Nuestro, dijo otra cosa (Pedo Nuestro). Y soltó ella la risa.

Pan con caca

Yo tuve una nieta murre atroz, ahi en el Rincón de las Mujeres. Juimos pallá pal Rincón, en la Jorupa. Le voy a platicar. Ahi teníanos labor—chile y de todo. Teníanos munchas verduras en Jorupa. Munchas cosas crecían, y dijo Crescencio, mi esposo,

—¿Por qué no llevas harina?

Y puso un horno de fierro. ¿Sabe qué es un horno de fierro? Ahi le puso brasas arriba. Lego me dijo,

—Curre dile a tu amá que amase.

Ya vino mamá y amasó y vino Crescencio y le echó lumbre. Le puso buñigas al horno. Buñigas. Lego otro día jue la Presila, mi nieta, y le dijo al mestro, a Juan Padilla,

—¡Oiga!—le dijo—. Mi granpo sabe hacer pan con caca.

—¿Cómo asina?

—Pus sí—le dijo—. Él puso las buñigas arriba del horno pa hacer pan.

Pus ea jue y le platicó al mestro. Era una pila de muchachos que jueron aá en casa, porque querían ver el pan de caca en Jorupa. Pero ésa (Presila) era murre atroz.

Basilio Gonzales
Gonzales Ranch, NM

▨ ¿Pa qué matates mi perro?

Una vez este perro había mordido una vaca de las vacas de nojotros. Yo traiba ganas de dale un balazo. Pos toca que estábanos yo y un primo mío ahi en la esquina de la casa y le dije,

—Ahi anda el perro y yo no tengo ni cartuchos.

—Yo traigo—me dijo.

Traiba cartuchos él. Metió la mano a la bolsa, y vine y saqué el veinte y dos yo. Le tiré un balazo al perro junte el represo, ahi junte el camino.

Pues entonces vino mi padrino. Era de mi padrino el perro. Vino aquí a en casa y me dijo,

—¿Pa qué le tirates un balazo a mi perro?

—Yo no le tiré a su perro.

—Pus alguien le tiró. Le dieron un balazo.

—Yo no sé quién le daría—le dije.

—Güeno—dijo mi padrino, y se jue.

Se jue onde estaba el otro muchacho. Era un primo mío. Jue y le dijo,

—¿Pa qué matates mi perro?

—Yo no ha matao su perro—dijo mi primo.

—Pus Basilio dijo que tú lo habías matao porque el cartucho es tuyo.

—¡Miente Basilio! Él lo mató. Yo nomás le empresté el cartucho, pero él lo mató porque el rifle es dél.

Pos no, no le pasó naa al perro. Nomás que mi padrino quería meternos miedo. Más tarde nos reímos yo y mi primo. Pero mi padrino estaba medio abusao quizás y jue y le dijo a mi primo que yo lo había matao.

¡El maiz es como la mentira!

Una vez andávanos yo y en papá sembrando maiz. Lo echábanos con la mano. Yo traiba un bote como de cinco libras y pa acabar pronto lo hice chorro en una carrera de un' orilla a lotra. Me dijo en papá,

—¿Sabes que hijo? ¡El maiz es como la mentira!

No puse atención. Yo sabía muy bien que es lo que quería entender. Pus cuando salió el maiz, me llevó pallá pa velo.

—¿Te acuerdas de lo que te dije hijo?—me dijo—. Mira que el maiz es como la mentira.

Salió too el maiz hecho chorro onde lo había sembraro yo. Como la mentira. Quizás una mentira si la dice uno, sale de algún modo, en algún tiempo.

Reynaldo Gonzales
Los Juertes, NM

Mi primer carro

Ya ni acordarme quiero, de ese carro, mi primer carro. A su papá de mi esposa le compré un carro. Loo el carro, pus, taa muy malo, hombre. Lo cambié por otro carro yo. Tamién ya estaa viejo el carro.

Pero yo tenía siempre mulas, caballos. Pus pa no trae los dos caballos pa subir la cuesta, porque estaa muy malo el camino, prendía una de las mulas adelante el carro. Le hablaba que lo jalara, que le ayudara al carro, y yo arriando el carro. Pus esta la mula no sabía naa. Estaa diatiro. Bien tapada. Me enojaba yo con la mula hasta que le enseñé. Ya sabía la mula. Le echaba la guarnición y la traiba atrás del carro hasta onde comenzaba a batallar el carro. Loo prendía la mula adelante. Le mandaba a la mula que jalara, que me ayudara con el carro, y yo arriando el carro. Cuando no quería entender, le daba sus fregazos a la mula. Hasta le daba peñascazos, garrotazos, y loo subía.

Loo le quitaba la guarnición a la mula y echaba la guarnición atrás en el carro. La mula se iba patrás pa la casa, pero el carro lo seguí teniendo ahi. Ya era mi segundo carro.

Luego ya había mestras de éstas que iban a dar escuela aá en el rancho. Pagaban por quien las trujiera de aá, pacá pa la Plaza (Las Vegas). Tenían que vinir que les pagaran o por comida. Pus eas pagaban renta aá. Renta onde estarse y too. Y me vido la mujer esa, muchacha era, que la trujiera. La truje yo. Ya el carro estaa muy viejo. Era techo de garra, ya muy pudrío. Pos cuando juimos de aquí (de la Plaza) pallá pal rancho, nos pescó una lluvia en el camino. Ahi vinía yo, y traiba a la muchacha esa yo, la mestra, y traiba otra muchacha. Usté sabe estas mujeres compraron trastes y quién sabe qué tanto. Pus se gotiaba el carro. De moo que se ponían las charolas aquí arriba la cabeza pa no mojarse.

Pero las llevé. Y ahi se acabó el cuento de mis carros. "Ya no" dije yo. "No, no más carro. No más andar lidiando con carros." ¡Compré mi primer troca!

Francisco Herrera
Antoñito, CO

▓ El vaquero

Había un vaquero que quería casarse con esta muchacha, y la muchacha no lo quería a él, y él no hallaba la manera de que se casara la muchacha con él.

Por fin consiguió a un hombre que se fuera a pasiar con él a la casa de la muchacha y que cuando él le dijera que tenía una cosa, que le ponderara que era más grande que lo que él dijiera. Cuando llegaron a casa de la muchacha, comenzó a contarle lo que tenía, y le dijo que tenía un ranchito, y le dice el otro,

—¡No ranchito, ranchote!

Y le dijo que tenía una casita, y le dice el otro,

—¡No casita, una casa muy grande, un palacio!

Y le dice que tenía unas vaquitas, y le dice el otro que vacales, no vaquitas. Y luego le dice que tenía unas borreguitas, y le dice el compañero,

—¡No borreguitas, borregales!

—Tengo unos caballitos.

—¡No caballitos, caballadas!

Tanto estuvo contándole lo que tenía, y la muchacha ya muy interesada y vía ella que no se sentaba a gusto, y le dice,

—Siéntese a gusto, señor.

—Si no puedo—le dice el vaquero—, tengo unas llaguitas de tanto andar a caballo.

Entonces le dice el compañero,

—¡No llaguitas, llagotas! Está hasta podrido.

Y ai sí se arrepintió la muchacha del todo y ya no se quiso casar con él.

Fred W. Korte
Buena Vista/Las Vegas, NM

Dos hombres cruzando un disierto

Le dice un hombre al otro,

—Espérame un ratito aquí. Tengo que ir a calcioniar.

Se fue detrás de un chamizo. Se bajo los pantalones. En eso llegó una víbora y le picó en el mero fundillo.

Llama a su amigo y le dice,

—¡Ay qué dolor amigo! Haz algo por mí.

Le responde el amigo,

—Yo no sé cómo curar el piquete de víbora.

Le contesta el compañero,

—Entonces ve de pronto al pueblo y dile a un doctor que estoy en clamor y grave dolor de piquete de víbora.

Pronto de galope fue al pueblo y vio a un doctor. Le contó al doctor lo allá del caso, y le preguntó qué podía hacer por su compañero. Le responde el doctor,

—No hay más que una sola cosa que puedes hacer. Afila bien tu navaja en una piedra y le haces dos cortes de esta manera (en forma de cruz) y le chupas el veneno con la boca.

Pronto regresó y cuando iba llegando, le preguntaba anciosamente su amigo,

—¿Qué dijo el doctor? ¿Qué dijo el doctor?

—Pues me dijo el doctor que no tenías cura. ¡Que tenías que morirte!

El telefón celular

Un hombre recibió un telefón celular para los Crismes. Le gustó tanto que todo el santo día lo usaba y en la noche hasta dormía con su telefón.

Un día le telefonió a su doctor que él estaba muy enfermo y no podía ir a verlo, pero que le mandara una medecina para sus dolencias de artritis. Le dijo el doctor que juntara los orines de una semana entera en un bacín y que se los mandara con su señora. Así él podía examinarlos y podía decidir qué medecina era la mejor para él.

Por una semana orinó en un bacín y como siempre traiba su telefón con él, accidentemente cáisele el telefón en el bacín. Pronto lo sacó del bacín y lo secó bien y pensaba que ya su telefón no iba a trabajar, pero siguió trabajando muy bien como siempre. Se puso muy contento.

Al fin de la semana ahi que va su señora con el bacín lleno de orines a llevarlos al doctor. Echó una travesía por un cerco donde había vacas. Con esta travesía en lugar de ser cinco millas al pueblo, había solamente tres millas.

Cuando iba pasando por este cerco, accidentemente trompezó con una piedra y volcó casi todos los orines. Se apenó mucho porque su marido se iba a enojar con ella. Pero en este tiempo vio a una ternerita que estaba orinando. Fue y le pusó el bacín y se volvió a llenarlo.

Y esos orines le llevó al doctor. A las dos semanas después, telefonió el doctor dándole su reporte. Le dijo que él estaba muy confuso con los resultados, que nunca en tantos años que él practicaba la medecina había tenido una causa como ésta. Y siguió,

—Pero yo chequié hasta seis o siete veces y sale la misma cosa. ¡No Hay Nada Duda! Usted está preñado de telefón, pero va a parir una ternera.

Anastasio Lobato
Antoñito, CO

▪ Los tres gachupines

Había unos tres gachupines que fueron a una suidá a aprender a hablar español. Estuvieron largo tiempo y no pudieron aprender más que uno a decir "nosotros," y el otro "porque quisimos" y el otro "justo es."

Una noche hubo una diversión en la plaza y mataron un hombre. Y a aquéllos les dio temor y salieron huyendo. Antonces el que sabía decir "justo es" iba adelante de los otros, el que sabía decir "porque quisimos" iba en el medio y el que sabía decir "nosotros" iba más atrás. Luego salieron los oficiales en pos de ellos. Cuando alcanzaron el primero, le preguntaron quién había matado al hombre. Dijo él,

—Nosotros.

Luego se vino el compañero que iba en el medio y le dijeron,

—¿Por qué?

—Porque quisimos—dijo él.

—Ahora será bueno matarlos a ustedes—dijeron los oficiales.

—Justo es—dijo el otro.

Edumenio Lovato
San Luis, NM

▨ Cayó una lluvia terrible

Te voy a platicar un cuento que platicaba mi agüelito. No sé si quedrás oílo o no. Pues una vez, más antes, que estaba muy seco, había muncho trigo. Ya se estaba secando el trigo. No tenía agua la gente y jueron y sacaron al Santo Niño. El Santo Niño de Atocha era una devoción muy especial que tenía yo cuando estaba joven. Y lo sacaron la gente en procesión. En esos tiempos lo llevaban pa los terrenos, a enseñale que se estaban secando los terrenos.

Pues esa noche después de que ya lo rezaron y todo, cayó una lluvia terrible. Y anegó todos los trigos; anegó todas las siembras. Las dejó por los suelos.

Pues otro día lo tiró la gente (al Santo Niño), los viejitos, y sacaron a María Santísima. La sacaron a María Santísima—y le enseñaban: "Mira la mierda que hizo tu hijo ayer después que le dijimos que nos diera agua."

Salomón Lovato
San Luis, NM

¿Por qué no pone los santos que escarden?

Esa Virgen que te ensené yo ai, cuando (Bernardino) Jovey se jue al *army*—*That was World First.* Su mamá la castigó. La tuvo en la petaquilla hasta que lo trujo patrás.

Y muncha gente, al Santo Niño más, lo castigaban. Es que decía la gente: "Puse el Santo Niño ai en tal lugar," y no estaba ai. Salía en otro lugar. Castigaban a los santos.

Loo también cuando sembraban ponían a San Antonio o a San Isidro en la era. Y un día le dijo un tío mío, era ya hombre grande, *he was a humorous man,* y no me acuerdo a quién, le dijo,

—¿Qué pusites los santos aá?

—Sí—le dijo—. ¡Pus es una seca bárbara!

—¿Por qué no pone los santos que escarden? ¡Qué está comiendo (la seca) la hierba!—dijo mi tío.

El padre no quería mis cinco pesos

Una vez estábanos en las fiestas de Cabezón, y estaba un amigo que se llama Avenicio Maestas. Él vive en San Ysidro. Y estaba un padre, Padre Leonardo. ¡Un hombre *German* grandotote! *He was rough!* Y estaba Avenicio en misa cuando pasó el padre el plato.

El pobrecito no traiba feria pero le dio cinco pesos y le dijo al padre,

—*Gimme the change it!*

No le dijo, "*Change it, Father!*" porque no sabía hablar inglés. Agarró los cinco pesos el padre y se los tiró. *We were in church, mind you!* ¡Unas risadas!

Loo salió Avenicio después de misa,

—Pus este padre—dijo—, no quería mis cinco pesos.

Juanita Malouff-Domínguez
Capulín/Chama, CO

Pidiendo posadas

Iba este hombre pidiendo posadas y le dijo al portero,

—Ando pidiendo posadas. ¿Qué me puede dicir?

—Allá está la mujer. Ve pregúntale a ella—dijo el portero.

Bueno. Va el hombre y se introduce con la señora, y le dice,

—Señora. Me llamo Pelos. Quiero preguntale si me quiere dar posadas. Ando pasiando por aquí y quisiera pasar la noche aquí.

—Güeno. Con gusto señor. Mi esposo llega más después, y ahora no creo que haiga ninguna problema de que pueda pasar la noche. Cenamos a las siete de la noche. Tenemos que estar invitaos.

Llega la hora de cenar y se sientan a la mesa. Como siempre está la hija, se sienta cerca la hija, y le dice el hombre,

—Señorita. ¡Mira que coincidencia! Estamos comiendo caldo de habas, y así me llamo yo.

Luego le dice la señorita,

—¡Mira que chistoso!

Siguen platicando y todo está bien. Llega el señor—el marido—más tarde, y le dice el hombre,

—Su esposa me dio posadas. Yo me llamo Chile.

—¡Bien venido!—le dijo el esposo.

Güeno. Se acuestan a medias de la noche. Empieza la niña, la hija,

—Caldo de Habas me está haciendo mal. Caldo de Habas me está haciendo mal.

Se levanta de la cama la mamá y le dice,

—¡Ves! Te dije que no comieras tanto.

Pero sigue la mamá pal cuarto y allí vido al malhechor y grita,

—¡Pelos entre las piernas de mi hija! ¡Pelos entre las piernas de mi hija!

Luego responde el padre,

—¡Déjala! Ya tiene la edá.

Pero luego jue allí el papá y vido lo que estaba pasando, y arranca a juir el malvado. Grita el papá,

—¡Agarren al Chile! ¡Agarren al Chile!

Se van todos contra él. Cuando llega el papá a la puerta ve al portero en el suelo y le dice,

—¿Qué estás haciendo en el suelo?

—¡Solo me di un fregazo pescando el Chile!

—Pos date otro por pendejo.

Unos barriles

Tenía este gringo unos barriles afuera de la tienda pa vender, y llegan estos dos hombres y dice uno de ellos,

—¡Y qué buenos barriles pa hacer vino! Mira, mira que buenos barriles. ¿Los quedrá vender el gringo?

—No sé. Yo le hablo. Yo sé hablar inglés—y va uno de ellos y le habla.

—Señor. *Sir*, que si le vende este barril a mi amigo.

Y le dice el gringo,

—*I don't know. I don't know.*

Y loo va patrás el hombre y le dice a su amigo,

—Dice que el barril sí lo vende, pero los aros no.

—Ah, ¡pus pa qué quiero el barril sin los aros!

La chamba

Éste es de dos señores que vinieron de México. Andaban buscando chamba. Eran músicos. Llegaron a Denver. Ahi andaan con el violín y la guitarra y se subieron en el tranvía. Luego viene el manejador—el conductor—y les dice,

—*Token please.*

—¡Ay, amigo!—dijo uno d'ellos—. Ya nos hallamos chamba—y empezaron a tocar.

Mi cuñada

Mi cuñada contaba la historia que no sabía cómo hablar inglés. Y un día se desmayó la niña que estaba sentada atrás d'ella en la escuela. Loo le dice mi cuñada a la hermana, a la hermana religiosa, a la maestra,

—*Sister, sister! She's smiled, she's smiled!*

Y le dice la hermana,

—*That's nice.*

—*No, no! She smiled!*

Al fin reconoció la hermana que la niña estaba desmayada.

Así hablaba ella inglés

Había esta señora que siempre iba a visitar a mi mamá. Siempre andaba con lo de *"The old man, sheck and sheck it!"* (*Shake it and shake it!*). Así hablaba ella el inglés porque no podía hablar inglés. Dicía ella *to the old man,*

—*Sheck and sheck it.*

And the old man says,

—*Lift up your dress and take it.*

Pos estaban juntando manzanas, pero la gente creiba que estaban haciendo otra cosa.

El sordo

Este hombre llegó caminando, pidiendo posadas. Llegó a esta casa y pidió posadas. Tocó la puerta, y le dijo la señora,

—Sí, le damos posadas. Tendrá que dormir en el suelo, pero está frío y le daremos que comer—le dice—. Nomás que mi esposo está muy sordo. Va tener que hablar muy, muy recio pa que lo oiga.

De modos que lo introdució ella a su esposo, y les dijo el que vinía pidiendo posadas,

—Muchas gracias, muchas gracias por darme posada.

Bueno, pues, platicaron un poco. Cenaron y se acostaron. Y se acostaron temprano como hacían más antes. Luego se hincó el que andaba pidiendo posadas, y empezó a rezar. Y dice,

—Cuando ya el sordo se duerma y lo sientas bien dormido (a la esposa), te levantas de tu cama y ya vienes y te acuestas conmigo. Y no se te olvide, y no se te olvide.

Y le dice el sordo a su mujer,

—Mira, viejita, ¡qué buen cristiano!

Cruz Márquez
Conejos, CO

Los dos rancheros

Era(n) don José María y don Antonio. Vivían cerca uno del otro y tenían animales y vendían mantequilla, blanquillos, carne y leche. Pues ellos los dos rancheros se decían compadres. En una vez llegaron unos americanos. Ese hombre José María no sabía absolutamente una palabra de inglés. Ya le dijieron los americanos que les vendiera blanquillos y leche. Él se entendió como pudo con ellos, con señas. Y le dice el americano al hombre que al otro lado del rito van a dormir, que otro día vaya por su pago. Pues no sabiendo él inglés, le dice él a su mujer,

—Voy a ver a mi compadre pa que vaya interpretarme. Él sabe muy bien el inglés.

Pues ya parte y se va para allá. Y le dice,

—Pues yo vengo a decile que llegaron unos americanos ayer tarde a en casa y me compraron leche y blanquillos. Como pudimos nos entendimos y dijieron que ai iban a dormir y ai están. Hora quiero que vaya conmigo pa que me vaya a interpretar.

—Muy bien—le dice don Antonio—. Vamos.

Y le dice don Antonio a los americanos, cuando llegan,

—Gur morning (*Good morning*), gringos ladrones. Al *pay* mi compadre José María. *You* no al *pay* mi compadre José María. *I'll breque* (*break*) *your* neque (*neck*) con un palo esteque (*stick*).

Bueno, el americano no podía entender, pero al fin le pagó y cuando iban en el camino, le dice don José a don Antonio,

—Si no ha sido por usté, no me pagan los americanos.

—Yo—le dice don Antonio—sé el inglés perfectamente—. No me avergüenzo en hablarlo.

Benerito Seferino Martínez
Trujillo, CO/Farmington, NM

▨ Don Cacahuate y Doña Cebolla

Don Cacahuate y doña Cebolla en un tiempo eran muy pobrecitos y no tenían dinero. No tenían dinero pa nada, y doña Cebolla estaba fregándolo la pacencia que quería ir a pasiarse, pero no tenían dinero. Al fin don Cacahuate se cansó de oíla y le dijo,

—Bueno, vamos a pasiarnos.

Y le dice ella,

—¿Cómo vamos ir? ¿Cómo vamos a pagar? Pos no tenemos dinero. No tenemos conque movernos.

Y le contesta él,

—No te fijes. No va costar nada. El paso está libre.

—¿Y cómo vamos ir?—le pregunta doña Cebolla.

—Pos, espérate. Yo te digo.

De modo que alistaron el lonche y las mochilas, con la ropa y todo. Se jueron al rumbo del ferrocarril. Agarraron todo el traque. Loo le dijo ella,

—¿Qué no dijites que íbanos a pasiarnos?

Aquí vamos. Aquí vamos de paseo.

—¿Qué no dijites que íbanos ir también de un modo fácil?—dijo ella.

—Sí, aquí vamos en un modo fácil. Vamos todos los traques, como el ferrocarril.

Y le dice doña Cebolla,

—¿Qué no dijites que también no tenemos dinero? ¿Cómo vamos a pagar el paso del tren?

—No te fijes viejita. ¡Aquí no te va cobrando naide!

La motocicleta

Una vez también estaban muy pobrecitos don Cacahuate y doña Cebolla, y no tenían en qué moverse. Al fin no sé cómo vino él y compró una motocicleta. Ahi va muy faceto a la casa y le enseñó a doña Cebolla la motocicleta. Y le dice,

—Vamos a tomar un paseo aquí por el camino.

Como en ese tiempo habían salido los carros, los carros andaban en el camino y las motocicletas también. En ese tiempo no estaban muy anchos los caminos. No había dónde pasarse otro carro de modo que al fin doña Cebolla dijo,

—Bueno. Yo voy a pasiarme contigo.

Ahi iban en el camino y se les hizo oscuro, de modo que vino don Cacahuate y prendió la luz de la motocicleta. Ahi van muy facetos pasiándose, con *air-conditioner* en la motocicleta. Bueno, y luego a la distancia vieron dos luces venir, y le dijo él,

—Cuide, doña Cebolla, lo que voy hacer. Voy a pasar entre esas dos motocicletas y los voy a asustar.

Y se van acercando más y más hasta que al fin le dijo don Cacahuate,

—¿Buena? ¿Lista? Aquí voy entre las dos motocicletas.

Cuando redepente, ¡pam! Era un carro. ¡No dos motocicletas!

Ice Cream

Cuando estaba joven don Cacahuate, se fue al servicio, a la guerra. Se tardó cuatro o cinco años pa volver. Y como entonces no había telefones, no había correo, o televisiones, doña Cebolla no sabía nada de don Cacahuate que estaba en la guerra, en el servicio. A los cuatro o cinco años, volvió don Cacahuate y ya doña Cebolla tenía un niño de cuatro o cinco años.

Bueno, todo pasó muy bien y le preguntó don Cacahuate,

—Oiga, doña Cebolla. Ese niño, ¿de dónde vino?

—Pues ya verá, don Cacahuate. Ora que no estaba usté aquí, compré *ice cream* y comí *ice cream*, y seguro que vino del *ice cream*.

Un día don Cacahuate decidió que iba ir a truchar y le dijo a doña Cebolla,

—Yo creo que llevo al niño, al niño del *ice cream*, a que aprenda a pescar.

Dijo doña Cebolla,

—Ah, seguro que sí. Tiene que aprender a truchar.

Bueno, pues se fue don Cacahuate en la mañana con el niño a pescar. En la tarde volvió con las truchas y los botinetes que pescaron, pero el niño no volvió a la casa. Al fin le carcomió doña Cebolla.

—Don Cacahuate. ¿Qué pasó con mi hijo? ¿Dónde está? ¿Por qué no volvió con usté?

Y le contestó don Cacahuate,

—Pues ya verá doña Cebolla. Como era hecho de *ice cream*, y con tanta calor, y tanto sol, ¡se reditió!

El espejo

Bueno, pues, don Cacahuate y doña Cebolla tuvieron un hijo. Al pobre hijo lo llamaron al servicio. En ese tiempo todavía no había munchas cosas. Todavía estaban inventando munchas cosas. Allá donde andaba el hijo halló un espejo y dijo, "Pues nosotros no tenemos uno d'esos allá en la casa. Tenemos que ir al río para poder vernos. Yo lo voy a comprar y lo voy a mandar pa la casa."

Al fin después de unos dos, tres años, que estaba el hijo en el servicio, recibieron ellos el espejo. Don Cacahuate es el que lo sacó del correo. Cuando llegó a la casa, le dijo doña Cebolla,

—Pues abre el parquete pa ver qué hay en el parquete.

Pues don Cacahuate se puso abrir el parquete y al fin lo abrió. Ahi estaba mirándolo [el espejo], y se soltó llorando don Cacahuate. Y doña Cebolla le dicía,

—Pues, ¿por qué lloras? ¿Por qué lloras? ¿Por qué lloras?

Y dicía don Cacahuate,

—¡Ay, el pobre! Pues estoy llorando por mi hijo. Mira que viejo se hizo.

Y doña Cebolla al fin le dijo,

—¿Pus qué mandó nuestro hijo un retrato o qué? ¿Por qué lloras, que está tan viejo? Da. Dame el retrato pacá.

Pues nada. Loo doña Cebolla vido el espejo y se nojó con don Cacahuate.

—¿Y por esta tal …,—y le echó unas palabrotas—. ¿Y por esta tal lloras tú?

▨ A Denver

Cuando don Cacahuate y doña Cebolla vivían en México, también estaban muy pobres. Al fin, pues, decidieron, "Si nos mudamos podemos hacer mejor vida." Ahi estuvieron pensando y pensando y pensando hasta que al fin le dijo don Cacahuate a doña Cebolla,

—¿Cómo le parece si nos mudamos a Denver?

Y le dice ella,

—¡Pues yo ni sé dónde queda Denver!

—Yo no sé tampoco. Yo no sé dónde quedará Denver, pero seguimos el mapa, seguimos el camino—le dice él.

Bueno, pues, todo pasó bien. Pasaron El Paso y de ahi Las Cruces y se vinieron a Alburquerque, Española, y entraron a Colorao. Y ahi iban muy contentos y "que ya mero llegamos." Ellos traiban todos sus muebles en la troquita que habían comprao para mudarse. Y ahi iban. Llegaron a Colorado Springs. Todo iba muy bien. Vieron un *sign* que dicía, "Denver, 100 millas." Ahi se pusieron muy alegres y se pusieron a cantar: "El Rancho Grande," "La Cucaracha," y asina. Iban cantando muy contentos.

Bueno, ya se iban acercando más y vieron un *sign* que dicía, 50 millas y luego otro, 25, y loo 10 y loo 5. Iban muy contentos. Ahi iban too el camino en la troquita—la troquita llena de muebles—cuando vido don Cacahuate un *sign* ahi y paró y se ladeó del camino. Paró la troquita y se puso a llorar. Doña Cebolla no sabía qué pasaba y le dicía,

—Don Cacahuate, don Cacahuate, ¿por qué llora?

Y doña Cebolla como no sabía leer estaba ahi queriendo consolarlo y queriendo hacerle la pregunta, "¿por qué lloras?," pa que le respondiera don Cacahuate, pero él no podía decir nada. Ahi estaba llorando, limpiándose la baba, las lágrimas y queriendo agarrar el resuello. Y le apuntaba a doña Cebolla, pero doña Cebolla no sabía leer. Y el pobre siguía llorando, llorando, llorando, hasta que al fin pudo decirle, ahi entre sollozos.

—Denver *Left*.

Y loo doña Cebolla le dice,

—Bien sabe que yo no sé hablar ni leer el inglés. ¿Qué contiene ése? ¿Qué quiere dicir?

Y le contesta él,

—Pues salimos mal, doña Cebolla.

—¿Por qué?—dice ella.

—Porque dice Denver *Left*. Denver se fue. De modo que no lo podemos hallar.

Estefanita Q. Martínez
De Tierra (Gonzales Ranch), NM

¿Quién mató el gallo?

Ora verás tú. Habían llegao don Julián Chávez y doña Conchita a case de mi agüelita y me dijo ella,

—¡Quítate pallá hijita! ¡Siéntate! Vete pallá afuera a jugar.

Antonces no lo dejaban a uno pasar por en medio de la gente como pasa ora. Loo le dije,

—Güeno. Orita me voy—, pero siempre me pasé por en medio. Dijo mi agüelita,

—Nomás se va la gente, nos vamos a comer el gallo.

Yo pensando me salí pa fuera muy contenta. Me senté en unos pinitos que estaban en la orilla de la casa. Loo dije, "No, pus mi *gramma* dijo que quería gallo pa cenar. Yo voy ir a matar el gallo. Ya pa cuando se vaya la gente está listo." Lo metí al cerquito de las gallinas y le di en el pescuezo hasta que ya lo maté. Vine y se lo truje a mi tía y le dije que mi agüelita quería comer gallo nomás se iba la gente. Loo la probe de mi tía fue y lo llevó pa un cuartito y lo peló bien y las plumas las puso abajo del cajete.

Yo me quedé saleriándome allá fuera hasta que se fue la gente. Loo dijo mi agüelita a mi tía,

—¡Llámela pacá. ¿Qué estaba pasando con el gallo? Esta malcriada le voy a pegar.

Vine y le truje el gallo de allá del cuarto ese que tenía y le dije,

—¡Aquí está, mire, pa comer carne pa la cena!

Se dio una güelta, me miró y loo dijo,

—¡Ven acá! ¿Qué andabas haciendo? ¿Quién mató el gallo?

—Cuando pasé delante de la gente me dijites, 'nomás se va la gente nos vamos a comer el gallo.'

Yo la tonta, pendeja fui y le maté el gallo. ¡Y la risa que me daba a mí! La risa que le daba a mi agüelita. Le dijo a mi tía,

—¡Cookéyalo hijita! ¡Échalo! ¡Y no te rajes!

No, pus nomás se fue la gente y comimos carne. ¿Y sabes que no me hizo nada mi agüelita. Me salvé de la friega?

Cesaria Montoya
San Pablo, NM

▦ Usté y un pendejo, muy poco la diferencia

Pus de chistes güenos, yo no me acuerdo de niuno. ¡Puros chistes puercos! Vale más ni dicilos porque ...

Una vez iba este hombre a caballo, y estaba este otro hombre, un viejito, escardando su maiz, lo que tenía sembrao. Y llegó el hombre de a caballo y le dice,

—Güenos días le dé Dios.

—Güenos días le dé Dios.

—¿Qué, qué está haciendo?

—Pus aquí—es que le dijo—, escardando mi milpita.

—Pero que seca está—le dijo—. ¿Por qué está tan amarilla? ¿Por qué está tan amarillo el maiz?

—Porque era maiz amarillo el que sembré.

Ya empezó el hombre a caballo a preguntale cosas asina y el viejito a respondele del mismo modo hasta que le dijo el de a caballo,

—Oh—le dijo—, usté y un pendejo, muy poca la diferencia.

—Sí—le respondió el viejito—, ¡nomás el cerco está de por medio!

Filimón Montoya
Cañón de Fernández (Taos), NM

▪ Don Cacahuate

Bueno, don Cacahuate y doña Cebolla no eran un *couple*. No tenían familia. Pero se iban de un pueblo al otro. Andaan con sus garras ahi y sus mochilas en el hombro.

—Y nos vamos ir por traque—le dijo él.

Y doña Cebolla entendió que iban ir en el tren. Isque le dijo don Cacahuate,

—Porque yo tengo el paso libre.

No le aclaró verdaderamente. No le aclaró que iban ir a pie caminando en el traque.

—Por traque—le dijo él.

Pero ea lo entendió mal. Ahi van hasta que ya a mediodía iba muy cansada la señora Cebolla. Loo le dijo ella,

—Oiga don Cacahuate, pus, ¿qué no dijo usté que tenía el paso libre?

—¿Pus quién le va cobrando, señora?

142

José Nataleo Montoya
San Pablo, NM

Prudencio Santillanes

Había un Prudencio Santillanes. Así se llamaba él. Era d'estos enbusteros, pero era como en una televisión él, ¿sabe cómo? Con tal de oyelo, pus la gente se recogía a oyer sus mentiras que les echaba él, ¿ve?

En una vez, que me acuerdo, de ahi de San Gerónimo se jue él pa San Isidro. En una burra se jue pallá. Quién sabe qué negocio tendría o a pasiarse o algo. Pus de allá cuando regresó, la comadre en San Isidro le mandó a su comadre aquí un queso. Él amarró un saco, un costalito en la silla de la burra que traiba. En un lugar que le dicen Corral de Encino, por onde vinía el camino en esos años, esque por ahi se enredó el queso. Pus cuando llegó aquí a San Gerónimo, no traiba el queso. Que llegó y le dijo su señora,

—¿Qué pasó? ¿Cómo te fue? ¿Bien? ¿Cómo están mi compadre y mi comadre?

—Pus están bien. Oh—le dice—, ¿sabes que te mandó un queso?

—¿Sí?—dijo su señora.

Ya él jue paá pa onde estaa la burra y jalló una hebra, como una hebra de hilo.

—Mira—le dijo—. Pus este queso se enredó por ahi.

Antonces vino y agarró la hebra esa aquí en los dedos y se jue haciendo la bolita, bolita hasta aá en el Corral de Encino. Aá completó el queso.

¡Que se vaya al infierno!

Ésta es la historia de Tomás. Pus tocó que perdió la mujer él, pero cuando vivía con ea, era muy malo con ea. La golpiaba y la regañaba y de todo. La maltrataba de toas maneras. Tocó que se murió ea, y quedó solo él.

Pus ahi comenzó a trabajale la mente y dijo, "Eh. Tan malo qu'era yo con mi esposa. ¿Cómo la estará pasando ahora? A la mejor no jue al cielo, pero yo voy a ver la manera a ver si encuentro alguien que me pueda ayudar a llevala al cielo."

¡Pues sí! Ahi se anduvo, navegando pallá y pacá hasta que halló a una señora que le habló a él. Supo que ea podía hacer d'esa clas de trabajo. Y la vido. Habló con ea y too. Se arreglaron.

—Sí—le dijo—, yo la llevo al cielo. Nomás que tráigame cincuenta pesos, y vuelva en siete días.

Pues sí. Le dio cincuenta pesos y se jue. A los siete días volvió, y nomás la vido y le dijo,

—¿Cómo le ha ido?

—Oh, bien. ¿Sabe que ya la encontré?

—¿De veras?

—Sí, de veras.

—¿Y cómo está?

—Está poco bien, pero está muy lejos del cielo tavía.

—Antonces, ¿cómo vamos hacer hacela llegar al cielo?

—Pus, tráigame otros cincuenta pesos y vuelva en siete días.

Ahi lo tuvo. Ahi lo tuvo por vario tiempo con sus cincuenta pesos y siete días hasta que una vez vino y llegó él y la halló a la señora muy fatigada, muy cansada a ea.

—¿Qué pasa?

—¡Ah!—le dijo ea—. Ando tan cansaa. Ha trabajao tanto, pero ora sí, su señora está tres pies de la puerta del cielo.

—¿De veras?

—Sí. ¡De veras que sí!

—¿Y ora cómo le vamos hacer?

—Pus déme otros cincuenta pesos, y la enboco al cielo.

—¡No!—le dijo el esposo—. Ya si no puede brincar tres pies, ¡que se vaya al infierno!

Katarina Montoya
El Ojo (Taos), NM

▪ Juan Cuchillete

Eran dos hermanos, y uno era muy, muy águila, y el rey era su padrino de uno d'eos, de Juan Cuchillete. Él era el abusao. El otro hermano estaa más joven. Le dijo el rey a éste,

—Te vas a quedar con mi madre hoy. Tienes que dale atole; no la vayas a dejar que tenga hambre. Le das suficiente atole.

Pus el muchacho estaa más tonto. Le embocó tanto atole hasta que l'ahogó a la viejita. Cuando vino Juan Cuchillete a casa y supo de la madre del rey, le dijo a su hermano menor,

—Ora verás te tú lo que vamos hacer. La vamos a componer muy bonita y la vamos a parar en la puerta. Loo tú vas y le dices a mi padrino que lo quiero ver.

Pus jue el rey y cuando abrió la puerta, cáese la viejita. Diuna vez brincó Juan Cuchillete y le dijo al rey,

—¡Mire lo que hizo con su madre! ¡Ya la mató!

a pedir. Tú vas a sanar a muncha, muncha gente. Y eso va estar bueno, pero te voy a dijir. Cuando tú llegues a la casa que vas a curar a la persona, si yo estoy en la cabecera, eso es que no quiero que la cures. Les dices que no puedes. Les dices que no sabes lo que tiene.

—Oh, sí, madrina. Yo haré todo lo que usté me dice.

Se fue ella y el muchacho comenzó su oficio. Era muy güen dotor. Dondequiera lo llamaban. Por muncho tiempo curó a muncha gente.

Una vez había un rey en el reinado, y vinieron los vasallos. Los trabajadores del rey. Vinieron a onde vivía el dotor. Este rey estaba enfermo y querían ellos que fuera a curarlo. Le daban muncho, muncho más dinero, más de lo que estaba haciendo. Güeno, pues se fue con ellos. Cuando llegaron allá estaba el rey en su reinado. Y su cuarto muy adornao. Lo primero que vido el dotor cuando entró al cuarto era su madrina. "Ay," es que dijo, "esto va estar muy trabajoso."

No, pues miró al rey y les dijo a los vasallos,

—No creo que puedo hacer nada por el rey, porque ya está muy enfermo. Y no, no va sanar.

—No, que yo te pago y te doy tanto de mi terreno. Te pago muncho dinero—le dijo el rey. "¡Ay!" es que dijía el dotor. "¿Cómo le haré?"

Al fin les dijo,

—Sí. Pues tráiganme una rondanilla. Pónganla aquí, y cabresto allá.

Vino el dotor y jaló la cama y la volteó. Pues quedó comadre Sebastiana en los pies. El dotor en un ratitito curó al rey. Ahi, estuvo, pues sanó. Se fue pa la casa el dotor, con muncho dinero y muy contento. Curó muncha más gente.

Cuando ya era señor lo volvieron a llamar a otro reinado. Éste estaba más lejos. También el rey estaba muy, muy enfermo. Cuando llegó allá el dotor, la misma cosa. Nomás entró al cuarto y en la cabecera estaba su madrina. Le hacía ella con la cabeza que no. Y él es que dijía, "Uh, hum." Pues, no. Prontito les dijo cómo le hicieran, y volvió a voltiar la cama el dotor. Se jue del reinado con mucho dinero. Ahi se anduvo curando.

Al fin un día vino su madrina. Vino a velo.

—Ay, madrina. ¿Cómo está?

—Bien, hijito, ¿y tú?

—Oh bien, madrina. Ha estao muy ocupao.

—Ah, como miro yo hijito, has estao muy ocupao.

—Amos a un paseo. Vamos conmigo porque yo quiero platicar contigo mi hijito.

—Sí, madrina. Bueno, vamos.

Luego lo llevó pa un lugar. Entraron pa dentro en esta casa. El suelo estaba todo tapado de velas. Estaban unas grandes, unas chiquitas, pero estaban todas prendidas. Le dijo él,

—¡Oh madrina! ¿Qué es esto?

—Mi hijito. Ésta es toda la gente que vive en el mundo.

—¡Oh!—dice él—. Unas están altas, otras están chiquitas.

—Sí. Las altas son los niños que ha nacido ahora. Las otras son las que ya se van haciendo ancianos.

Antonces voltió él par onde estaba una chiquitita.

—Y ésta madrina, ¿qué es?

—Ésa eres tú—y apágase la vela y muérese el dotor. ¡Y ahi estuvo!

El rey y la princesa

—Pues yo no sé la princesa por qué no se ríe. Quizás está enferma—dicía el rey.

Ella no se reía ni nada. Pues la llevaron pa todos los dotores, y no. No, no tenía nada. Nomás no se podía reír.

Luego pues puso el rey un aviso en el periódico y el muchacho que pudiera hacer a la princesa reír, le daba su mano pa que se casara con ella. Le daba la mitá del reinado. Oh, pus, vinieron munchos y munchos muchachos. Pero naide la hizo reír. Le contaban toda clase de chistes, y quién sabe qué tanto.

Al fin estaba un muchacho muy simple. Él oyó dijir que estaban dando a la princesa, quien la pudiera hacer que se riyera. Le dijo él a su mamá,

—Pues yo voy a ir.

Le dice su mamá,

—No. ¿Pues qué vas a poder hacer tú? Mira cuántos han venido y no

149

la han hecho que se ría.

Pues cayó allá él, y estaba la princesa sentada. Andaban las camareras sirviendo, cosas pa beber. Andaban sirviendo té. Y le dijieron al muchacho,

—¿Quieres un vaso de té?

—¡Oh, sí!—les dijo él.

Él estaba sentao en esta mesa y la princesa estaba en l'otro lao. Loo volvió a vinir la camarera a ver si quería más té, y le dijo él,

—Sí, quiero más.

Al fin, se paró la princesa, y le preguntó que si quería más té.

—¡Oh sí! *Entre más té bebo*, más té quiero*—y es que a la princesa le dio aquella risa.

—Olas, solas—dijo el rey—. ¿Pues con quién se ríe mi hija?

—Él (el muchacho simple) la hizo rir—dijo una de las camareras.

—Pues le voy a dar la mano pa que se case con ella.

Se casó con la princesa y garró parte del reinado.

*La princesa confundió "té bebo" por "te bebo"

Juan Manuel Olivas
San Pablo, CO

El católico y el judío

Este católico y un judío estaban trabajando en un disierto. El católico trabajaba por el ferrocarril. El judío trabajaba por las norias de aceite. A menudo se topaban y se ponían a desafiarse a ver cuál tenía mejor trabajo. El judío dicía, "pues, nosotros garramos este sueldo y luego nos pagan. Tenemos ciertas protecciones." El ferrocarrilero dicía que tenían casi las mismas protecciones. Una por otra salían poco más o menos cerca.

Pero en una ocasión jue el judío a la Plaza y compró un camioncito nuevo y llegó donde estaba el católico y le dice,

—Mira lo que yo hice. Esto porque tengo güen trabajo y compré un camioncito nuevo.

Güeno. Como a la semana, semana y media, jue el católico tamién a la Plaza y se compró un automóvil nuevo. Cuando volvió le dijo al judío,

—Mira. Tamién yo compré automóvil nuevo y tamién con el trabajo del ferrocarril. Vamos a un paseo.

Se jueron. Había como treinta millas al pueblo. Jueron allá. Cuando llegaron le dijo el católico al judío,

—Ya me voy patrás. Tengo que ir a ver al sacerdote—y se jueron.

Luego salió el sacerdote y le dijo al católico,

—Tengo muncho gusto que compraras un vejículo nuevo y voy a bendicilo—y agarró agua bendita.

El judío nomás lo miró, pero no sabía de qué se trataba todo aquello. Cuando volvió patrás pal ferrocarril el católico, se vino el judío muy calladito al sitio de las norias de aceite donde trabajaba. El judío toavía pensar y pensar. Al ratito llegó él y le tocó la puerta al católico. Vinía el judío con un *hacksaw* y un pedacito de *tailpipe*. Loo le dijo al católico,

—Mira. Tú pensates que tú sabías más que yo.

—No—le dijo el católico—. No. ¿Por qué?

—Tú llevates a tu vejículo que lo bendiciera tu ministro. Pos mira lo que hice con el mío. ¡Lo hice *circumcized*!

■ Un borracho

No sé qué sermón estaría echando el padre, cuando de repente les dijo a todos,

—Si no hacen estas cosas, se van ir todos al infierno. Se van a condenar. Loo les dijo,

—Los que no se quieran condenar, siéntense.

Y estaba un borracho en misa y no se fijó lo que había dicho el padre. Se sentaron todos. Luego le dijo el borracho al padre,

—¡Oiga! Yo creo que nomás yo y usté nos vamos a condenar, porque los demás ya se sentaron.

Julia B. Olivas
Pueblo, CO

■ Te vamos a buscar mujer

Un chiste que me contó mi esposo es de un matrimonio. Tenían un hijo. Güeno, el hijo ya tenía sus años—tenía treinta o treinta y dos años. Y es que una vez le dijieron,

—Mañana vamos a la plaza y te vamos a buscar mujer porque ya es tiempo de que te cases. Ya nosotros estamos muy viejos; nos muremos y te vas a quedar solo.

Otro día prendieron los caballos en el carro y se subieron y le dijieron que ya se iban a buscale una muchacha de treinta años. Güeno, se jueron y le dieron a los caballos. Y luego rompió corriendo el muchacho y dice,

—¡Espérenme! ¡Espérenme un poquito! Si no me jallan una de treinta, tráiganme dos de quince.

■ Me deja sin ver hijas

Havía una mujer y tenía dos hijas y trabajaban retirado dionde ella vivía. Venían en el tren a vela y se volvían patrás en el tren. Y cuando las hijas ya se iban, dicía la mamá,

—¡Oh! Este tren se lleva a mis hijas llorando, y a mí me deja sin ver hijas (verijas).

Antonia A. Ortiz
El Pueblo, NM

▨ Muy travieso el viejito

Lo que pasaba antes es que la mujer y el hombre—y ha pasao siempre—no conviene uno con lotro, ¿ves? Ahi es onde está too.

Platicaban antes que esque echaron a casar unos novios. Trujieron a un viejito. Estaba muy travieso el viejito. Él trujo un cabrestito; estaba muy bien tejido el cabrestito. No estaba cortao ni nada. Vino él y lazó al novio y le dijo,

—¡Vente pacá! ¡Párate aquí!

Loo le dijo a la novia,

—Y tú, ¡párate aquí!

Los lazó a los dos. Antonces le dijo al novio,

—¡Camina tú!

Eso enseñaban—que para onde se juera su marido, tenía que irse ella. Estaa curioso, ¿no?

▨ ¡Si yo ni lo conozco!

Mamá platicaba que cuando a ella la pidieron pa que se casara con mi papá, es que le dijo ella a su papá,

—¿Pero pus cómo quieren que me casé yo con ése? ¡Si yo ni lo conozco!

Es que le contestó él,

—¡Pero yo sí lo conozco!

Félix Pino
Santa Fe, NM

■ El padre y los blanquillos

Éste era un padre. Venía a dicir misa en un pueblito y tomaba la comida en casa de la mamá de Celestino. Un día que vino el padre a dicir misa, se le olvidó a la mamá de Celestino preguntale cómo quería que le hiciera los blanquillos, si con chile o solos. De ai a poco rato entró Celestino y le dice su mamá,

—¿Qué no fuites a misa, hijo?

—No—dice Celestino—, ya se me hizo tarde y no fui.

—Sabes que le voy a dar al padre de comer hoy a mediodía blanquillos y chile y se me olvidó preguntale si los quería en blanco o con chile.

—Yo voy a preguntale, mamá—le dijo Celestino.

—Pero ¿qué vas a ir, hijo, si ya están en misa?

—¿Qué le hace que estén. Yo veré cómo hago.

—Bueno, haz como tú quieras.

Entonces se fue Celestino para la iglesia y entró y vido que ya estaba el padre diciendo misa. Vino y se sentó bien, bien delante, donde el padre lo pudiera ver a él. Cuando vio que el padre se voltió para onde estaba la gente a dicirles, "Dominos obispo," tomó la palabra Celestino y le dijo,

—Pater, dice mi mater que si cómo le gustan los huevos, si en blancorio o chilorio.

Y le respondió el padre,

—Dile a tu mater que en blancorio, porque en chilorio me arde el século seculorio.

155

Elizardo R. Romero
Grants/Chacón, NM

La mentira más grande

En un tiempo se juntaban estos dos hombres a ver quién dijía la mentira más grande. Estaban los dos hombres y uno le dijo a l'otro,

—¿Sabes que al punto de aquel cerro está una hormiga?

Y le dice l'otro,

—¡Yo no la veo, pero siento los pasos!

Un toro bramando

Les pregunta este hombre a sus compañeros,

—Oigan, muchachos, díganme, entre dos paredes blancas pasó un toro bramando, ¿Quién sabe lo que de veras era el toro?

Ahi los tuvo en ayunas por muncho tiempo, pero no les quiso dicir qué era. Y ellos no sabían. ¡Era un pedo!

Un marrano

Éste es un cuentecito entre dos hombres. Uno le pregunta a l'otro,

—¿Qué hace más ruido que un marrano bajo diún cerco?

Y l'otro hombre se quedó pensando pero no supo cómo responder.

—¡Dos!—le dijo l'otro.

Alicia Romero-Vidaurre
Llano de San Juan Nepomuceno, NM

▪ En un tanto cuanto

Platicaba esta mujer ... Güeno, su marido se llamaba Juan y era mure parrandero. Le gustaba muncho beber. Se iba a la parranda y cuando volvía llegaba acabando con ella. Pegándole y maltratándola. Ya la pobre estaba bien aturdida. Bien atemorizada del mal trato que le daba.

Pus un día llegó de la parranda queriendo pescoliala pa meniale. La traiba al retrotero alredor de la mesa en la cocina. Corrían pallá y corrían pacá, él tirándole tarascadas queriendo pescala y ella juyéndole.

Pus isque estaba la llave de la estufa puesta en la tapadera. Más antes siempre había lumbre en las estufas porque las mujeres ponían comida a cocer y se tardaba todo el día pa cocerse. Pus se jaló la manga del cuerpo que traiba y agarró la llave de la estufa y se la puso ansina pa protegerse de él. Pus el tonto, atarantao, tira la tarascada y en wal de agarrala a ella, agarra la llave de la estufa y, ¡quémase la mano!

Pus ése jue su santo remedio. No volvió a pegale. Sí siguió parrandiando. Bebió hasta que se murió. Pero nunca volvió a pegale. A ella le encantaba platicar cómo lo había arreglao. "Sí," dijía, "en un tanto cuanto arreglé a Juan."

▪ El día que nací

Platicaba mamá que el día que nací, esa mañana se había ido muy temprano pa la Cuchilla Pelaa a regar la labor. En papá tenía tierras del dijunto Alejandrino contratadas y mamá era la que las beneficiaba. En papá estaba trabajando en Guayume, y mamá era la que se encargaba de las tierras. Ese año habían sembrao trigo, aveno, sebada, frijol, alberjón, habas, calabazas, maiz blanco, maiz amarillo, y maiz azul pa hacer atole y chaquegüe.

Pus esa mañana alistó lonche y se jue a pie, a regar. Y esas tierras estaban retiradas de la placita onde vivíanos. Croque como una milla, fácil que hasta más lejos.

Pus isque cerca de mediodía comenzaron a pegale los intuertos. Entre más y más juertes hasta que ya no aguantó. Dejó l'agua corriendo y se vino. Llegó a casa la dijunta Delfina avisale que andaba muy enferma y que juera pronto a llamar a la partera.

Allí en la placita onde vivíanos, pus estaban las casas bien apretadas unas con otras. Hechas chorro, de un lao y de otro. Pronto se sabía lo que pasaba. De modo que pronto llegaron las vecinas y las comadres y alistaron la cama y lavaron a mamá. Porque mamá cuando regaba se quitaba los zapatos pa no acabalos; regaba descalza. Pus isque traiba los pies hechos zoquete. Ellas como pudieron la lavaron y la metieron a la cama.

Trujieron leña partida. Pusieron agua a calentar y alistaron munchas garras. Ya cuando llegó la partera ya estaba todo listo. Y dijía mamá que en un tanto cuanto había sanao. Que no había batallao muncho. Pronto nací. Isque le dijían las que estaban allí, "¡Qué bárbara Matilde, a la güena si sanas allá entre las calabazas y el alberjón."

Alfredo Roybal
Mora, NM

Don Cacaguate y Doña Cebolla

Una vez estaba don Cacaguate y doña Cebolla caminando por el traque del tren cuando venía el tren. Le dice doña Cebolla a don Cacaguate que se moviera del traque porque venía el tren. Don Cacaguate corrió lejos del traque hasta que pasó el tren. Cuando volvío patrás le pregunta doña Cebolla que si por qué se fue tan lejos. Le contesta don Cacaguate que por si a caso venía el tren de lado.

La mala nota

Estaban tres hermanos: uno era banquero, otro músico, y el otro era un tontito (tartamudo) que vivía en un ranchito. Un señor les dice,

—Explíqueme qué es una mala nota.

Le dice el banquero,

—Una mala nota es cuando una persona va al banco por un préstamo, firma una nota por el dinero, pero no paga el préstamo. Ésa es una mala nota.

Le dice el músico,

—Cuando está tocanando la banda y uno de los músicos le pega a una nota que no va con la música, ésa es una mala nota.

Antonces le dice el tontito al señor,

—Una mala nota es cuando una malana (marrana) tiene muchos malanitos (marranitos). Ésa es una malanota (marranota).

Philomeno Sánchez
San Luis, CO

La pata culeca

Un domingo fueron mi compadre Pánfilo y mi comadre Sindicha al *flea market*, al mercado de pulgas, y compraron un par de patos. El pato y la pata. Como no los pudieron tener en la ciudad por largo tiempo, se los llevaron a sus padres porque ellos vivían en un ranchito.

Con el tiempo y un ganchito, la pata se hizo culeca cerca del río, y no dejaba a nadie que se arrimara cerca de ella. Un día vino su comadre Hizquepula a visitar a doña Perrimplina, y entre pláticas salió que ya la pata se había hecho culeca. Le dice doña Hizquepula,

—Sabe comadre que yo no conozco los huevos de pata.

Le dice doña Perrimplina,

—Vamos. Se los enseño. Si nomás que está tan brava esa pata ahora que está echada, que no nos deja arrimarnos. Pero espérese. Allá viene su compadre Pite. Déjeme pegarle un grito para que nos ayude.

Salieron las comadres, y le pega doña Perrimplina un grito,

—¡Oiga don Pite! Venga a levantarnos la pata, que mi comadre Hizquepula quiere conocerle los huevos.

Esta cabra tiene vergüenza

Pocos días después de que llegué a casa, me informaron que mi padre padecía de úlceras en el estómago. De remedio le habían dado que tomara leche de cabra en ayunas.

Comenzó mi padre a comprar leche de cabra en el comercio, pero a poco de tiempo pensó que sería más barato si compraba mejor la cabra que la leche.

Compró la cabra y la comenzó a ordeñar. Una mañana que me tocó levantarme de mañana, me fui para la caballeriza donde estaba ordeñando la cabra. Lo primero que noté que la tenía amarrada de una pata con un cabresto.

Le pregunto a mi padre,

—¿Qué éste es el estilo de hoy en día para ordeñar las cabras—de amarrale una pata?

Me dijo,

—No hijo, si le amarro una pata porque esta cabra tiene mucha vergüenza.

—¿Pero qué está hablando?—le dije yo—. Yo no he oido en mi vida que una cabra tenga vergüenza.

—Pues ésta sí tiene—me dijo—. Nomás la voy a ordeñar, y me tira patadas. ¡No me deja que le agarre las chiches!

▪ Sabiendo que son hasta ajenas

Como teníamos tantos amigos (él y su esposa) pronto entramos a la política. Como éramos políticos siempre andábamos en las convenciones. En la primera convención que estuvimos en la capital del estado, después de la comida salimos para la calle a un paseo. Nomás en cuanto habíamos caminado medio bloque y vimos que venían dos muchachas, pero guapas, tan lindas como Mona Lisa. Le digo yo a Elsie,

—Nomás mira qué pollas, y qué piernitas de amoles. Ésas no pueden mentir que no beben atole y comen frijoles. Y fíjate en esas *headlights*, lo que tú les nombras limones. Para mí parecen ser mejor coles . . .

Me dijo Elsie,

—¡A qué mi Phil O'Menito sin venas! ¿Por qué tan poquito te apenas . . . sabiendo que son hasta ajenas . . . de suerte no te condenas . . . y te cuelgan con unas cadenas . . . por querer traer las dos manos llenas . . . ? Ahora te voy a decir yo la cierta . . . espero que tú lo comprendas . . . por las cosas que ahora estás viendo . . . solito las estás sufriendo. Pero no te fijes en pollas culecas . . . fíjate en las que están poniendo . . .

Yo soy la que los tengo

Para el tiempo de la Depresión, a mi compadre Campeche y a mi comadre Nicanora se les puso el tiempo más tirante que un cerco de alambre de púa. Mi compadre cosía sacos, no con lumbre, sino que con una aguja en una fábrica. Pero en ese año inventaron una máquina que cosía veinte veces más rápido que él, y por eso lo desocuparon.

Por un año agarró compensación y estampillas. Luego tuvo que comenzar a robar para poderse alcanzar porque tenía tres hijos: el Lito, el Tito, y Benito. Después robaba porque decía que tenía necesidad. Al fin ya robaba por neciedad. Como tanto va el cántaro al agua hasta que al fin peca, así le pasó a mi compadre Campeche. Lo pescaron robando y lo despacharon a la pinta por veinte años.

Pronto aplicó mi comadre Nicanora por asistencia para los niños. Al cabo de dos años vino un representante del *Welfare Department* a revisar su aplicación. Cuando llegó a los números de niños, le dijo el representante a mi comadre Nicanora,

—Aquí dice en la aplicación que usted tiene cinco hijos. Cuando don Campeche se fue a la prisión, no tenía más que tres. ¿Cómo es eso?

—Sí, es muy cierto—le dijo mi comadre Nicanora—, pero debe de darse cuenta que él es el que están en la prisión. Yo no estoy. Y no sólo eso, él no los tiene. Yo soy la que los tengo.

Me privó el doctor el cigarro

Cuando estaba en el hospital me privó el doctor el cigarro. Un día andaba en la calle con tamaño cigarro cuando me encontró Chalito Mondragón y me dijo,

—¿Qué demontres tiene *Mister* Sánchez? ¿Qué no se escapó de morir de ataque de corazón? ¿Qué no le privó el doctor el cigarro?

—Sí me lo privó—le dije—. Por cuatro meses no lo toqué, pero cuando ya descansé, comencé con este vicio maldito y no lo puedo dejar.

—Si lo quiere dejar, yo le doy un remedio, y le aseguro que en dos días lo puede dejar—me dijo Chalito.

—Déme el remedio—le dije yo—. Con un remedio no me he de morir. Y si me toca morir con ese remedio, ya muerto no hay remedio. Un remedio, para una cosa que no tiene remedio, no sirve de remedio.

—Éste es el remedio—me dijo Chalito—. En la mañana para almorzar coma cuatro huevos fritos. En el medio días, los dobla. Coma ocho huevos fritos. En la cena, los dobla. Coma diez y seis huevos fritos. Otro día al almorzar, los dobla. Coma treinte y dos huevos fritos.

—Oh, ¿pero qué demonios voy hacer yo con tantos huevos fritos?—le dije yo.

—Ése es el secreto de mi remedio—le dijo Chalito—. Para dejar de fumar, ¡se necesitan muchos huevos!

Se me acabó la carrera de ser orador

Cuando tenía seis años de edad, entré a la escuela de un Santo en San Pedro. El Santo que según dicen supone tener las llaves del cielo.

Yo hubiera sido un rey Salomón para hablar en público, pues comencé desde muy mediano. A mí me gustaba aprender las poesías que la maestra nos enseñaba. Como nunca ha tenido vergüenza, siempre me gustaba pararme en frente de la clase a recitar una poesía. La más favorita, la que me gustaba más, era *"Mary Had a Little Lamb."*

Un día la maestra, la señora Andrea Medina, quería enseñarnos cómo era el modo más apropiado para hablar en público. Como yo era el más sinvergüenza, a mí se me dirigió y me dice,

—Sánchez, párese en frente de esta clase y díganos una poesía.

Como no tenía vergüenza, y como no la conocía, me paré tan tieso como un palo de teléfono y comencé con mi poesía favorita.

—*Mary had a little lamb.*

¡No, no, no, no!—me dijo—. No así. Cuando uno habla en público, tiene que expresar sus acciones de esta manera. Tiene que usar las manos. *"Mary had a little lamb," so you put your hands in front. When you say the next line, you put your hands in back like this.* ¿Comprende?

—*Yes, Mrs. Medina. I comprende*—le dije yo.

Hice una mediana tos, me limpié el gaznate, y con una voz ladina y clara, comencé diciendo,

—*Mary had a little lamb in front. His fleece was white as snow behind. And everywhere that Mary went in front, the lamb was sure to follow her behind.*

Yo no sé cuál sería la razón, pero toda la clase comenzó a reír. A mí me importó un pito, pero cuando vi que hasta la maestra se estaba riendo de mí, dije, "Ésta es la última vez que me paro enfrente de una clase. En mi vida no volveré a hacer un papalote de mí mismo."

Ese día en San Pedro se me acabó mi carrera o tal vez mi deseo de ser un orador público.

Eduardo Valdez
Guadalupe (Ojo del Padre), NM

▨ El botito del rey

Ésta es la historia de un rey, y este rey tenía una hija única. Y una viejita tenía un hijo único y la viejita era muy pobrecita. El muchacho cuando iba pa la estafeta—vivían en un rancho—pus siempre le gustaba comprar el pedióvico porque le gustaba lelo. Y este rey un día pensó casar a su hija y no podía decidir con quién.

Antonces es que dijo: "Voy a hacele asina. Voy a colgar un botito aquí en las vigas de este cuarto, y le voy a echar mierda y un grillito negro. Loo voy a poner un publicao en el papel de que el que venga y adivine qué tengo en ese botito, ése se casa con mi hija. Si no adivina, pena de la vida." ¿Ves?

Antonces el rey puso un publicao en el pedióvico, en el papel, del que que viniera y adivinara qué tenía colgao en ese botito, se casaba con su hija. Antonces este muchacho, el hijo de la viejita, agarró el papel y leyó este publicao. Cuando llegó a la casa, le dijo a su mamá, de que había hallao aquel publicao en el papel que había publicao el rey, que el que adivinara qué tenía él dentro del botito que tenía colgao en las vigas se casaba con su hija. Antonces le dijo el muchacho a la viejita que él quería ir a ver si adivinaba qué tenía el rey en el botito. La viejita no quería porque el que no adivinara, pus, lo mataba el rey. ¿Ves?

Antonces le dijo la viejita,

—¿Pus que quieres que te mate el rey?

—Pus no—esque le dijo—. Pero quiero ir a ver si adivino, a ver si me caso con la hija del rey.

La viejita nunca pudo convencelo que no juera. Al fin decidió la viejita de dale licencia que juera. Y le dijo,

—¡Anda, vete, grillito negro, adivinador de mierda, a que te mate el rey!

El muchacho todavía animao, se jue pallá, a ver si adivinaba qué tenía el botito. Pues cuando llegó allá a casa del rey, había munchos adelante, sabes, que estaban iyendo a ver si adivinaban, y ni uno adivinaba. Todos los estaba matando el rey, los estaba sacando y los estaba matando. Pues en fin, le tocó su tiempo a él. Su turno, como dijemos. Lo llamaron. Ya esque le dijo el rey, que si acuál era la causa de su visita. Ya le dijo él,

—Vide el publicao que puso en el papel, señor rey—esque le dijo—de que el que viniera y adivinara qué tiene colgao en ese botito se casaba con su hija. Y si no adivinaba, pus penaba de la vida. De modo que, que yo vine a ver si vivía o moría—esque le dijo el muchacho.

—Pues. ¡Ándale!—esque le dijo—. Párate pacá.

Ya esque se paró y le dijo el rey,

—¡A ver! Adivina a ver qué es lo que hay en ese botito. Y si adivinas, tú vas a ser mi yerno.

Antonces esque se acordó el muchacho de lo que le dijo la viejita, y esque se soltó llorando. Esque dijo,

—¡Válgame Dios! ¡Mal haya y cuando jui a venir! Bien me decía mi madre, "Grillito negro, adivinador de mierda."

—¡Hola!—le dijo el rey—. ¡Eso es lo que es!

Dos jóvenes que querían ser astrónomos

Éste es un caso que pasó con dos jóvenes que estudiaban y querían ser astrónomos. Un día salieron de la suidá al campo. Querían ver los astros del cielo y estudiar las estrellas y llegaron en casa de una viejita que vivía sola en un rancho. Esta viejita era muy pobrecita. No tenía más que un cuartito, y adelante del cuartito un cerquito donde tenía un burrito. Este burrito, cuando iba a llover, retozaba y se ponía muy contento, y la viejita ya sabía que iba a llover.

Los jóvenes le pidieron pasada y la viejita les dice,

—Jóvenes. No tengo más que este cuartito y nomás una cama.

Y les dijo que esa noche iba a llover. No importó. Los jóvenes le dijieron que ellos dormían allí afuera, que traiban sus camas y comida, y que ellos querían estudiar los astros del cielo porque estudiaban para astrónomos. La viejita les dice,

—Bien, cuando llegue la lluvia, entren aquí adentro para que no se mojen.

Los jóvenes se decían uno al otro: "¿Cómo sabe esta mujer que va a llover?"

—Pregúntale tú que te diga cómo sabe que va a llover cuando no hay ni nubes—dijo uno de ellos.

Antonces el otro de los jóvenes le preguntó,

—Señora, ¿cómo sabe usté que esta noche va a llover?

La viejita les dijo,

—¿Ven ese burrito en el cerquito? Cuando él retoza y está alegre, por cierto viene lluvia. No hay engaño.

A poco que oscureció, se comenzaron a poner nubes. En poco rato comenzó la lluvia y los jóvenes metieron sus camas al cuartito; llovió toda la noche. Por la mañana uno de los jóvenes mueve a su compañero y le dice,

—¡Levántate! Vamos antes que amanezca. Es una vergüenza que un burro sepa más que nosotros.

Y se fueron y la viejita se quedó dormida.

Floyd E. Vásquez
Chacón, NM

El bacín

Bueno, pus había una vez una pareja, y llegó la hora y vino él del trabajo. Llegó *halfway* adentro de la casa. La mujer estaba sentada y le dijo,

—Oyes, tú qué andas parao, menea las papas.

Fue él y meneó las papas. Entonces le dijo ella,

—Oyes, tú que estás parao, traeme las tortillas.

Fue él y trajo las tortillas.

—Oyes, tú que andas parao, traeme el café.

Trajo él el café. El golpe final fue cuando le dijo ella,

—Tú que andas parao, traeme la azúcar ora.

Y dijo él, "Ésta aprovechada. No puedo con esto," y se puso andar de rodillas. Se quedó así, y la mujer lo vido pero no dijo nada. Así se quedó él todo el resto del día, a rodillas. Caminando por toos laos. Muncho después cuando se iban acostar le dijo ella,

—Oyes, ¡tú que andas de rodillas saca el bacín!

Un padre

Vino a chequear el arzobispo en el padre. No sabía qué hacer el padre cuando vinía el arzobispo, el hombre más importante. Pues invitó el padre al ministro y se fueron los tres a cazar en la montaña. Pasando la noche, primero le dice el arzobispo,

—¡Ay! No sé qué decir, pero tengo tantas ganas de fumar. Ay, de fumar. Pero padre, yo la manía de fumar.

—¿De fumar? Pues, no pasa nada. Fume lo que quiera.

Al segundo, antonces el padre dice,

—A mí no. Mi vicio es el alcol. A mí me gusta muncho el *whiskey.* ¡Muncho! Pero la tequila es lo que me gusta pa emborracharme.

—Oh, pues aquí estamos desde mismo, hombre. Toma too lo que quieras.

Luego miraron al ministro, y no dijo nada.

—Pues, tú, ¿qué?—dijo el arzobispo.

—Oh, a mí no—respondió el ministro—. Lo que me gusta es mitotear.

Cruzita Vigil
Corazón, NM

La viejita y el viejito

¡Oh sí tengo este chiste del gallo! Güeno, isque había dos viejitos: la viejita y el viejito. Y tenían gallinas. Una mañana le dijo el viejito a la viejita,

—Ya ese gallo no sirve. Ya está muy viejo. Ya no pisa las gallinas. Voy a ver si jallo un muchacho.

Jue y trujo un gallo nuevo, y nomás vido el nuevo al viejo y se jue en pues del gallo viejo. Cuando vido los dos gallos entró el viejito muy apurao.

—Dame el rifle de ahi.

—Pus, ¿qué vas hacer?—le dijo la viejita.

—A matar ese gallo. Al igual de trai gallo, truje un joto.

San Pedro era compañero de mi Tatita Dios

San Pedro era compañero de mi Tatita Dios, y es tavía. Pero cuando ya se apartó mi Tatita Dios de San Pedro, que el día que ya se fue pa su Gloria, siempre fue San Pedro atrás de mi Tatita Dios. Abrió poco la puerta y le dijo el Señor,

—¿Qué andas haciendo aquí San Pedro?

—Naa. Vine a verte. Yo no me quiero separar de Ti.

Y se fue enbocando poco a poco, poco a poco. Se jue enbocando poco a poco San Pedro, hasta que se metió pa dentro sin dejalo mi Tatita Dios. Cuando ya estaa adentro le dijo mi Tatita Dios,

—Ya, ya entrates San Pedro, pero te volverás piedra.

Ya le dijo San Pedro,

—¡Pero con ojitos!

GLOSARIO

Much of the Spanish dialect of northern New Mexico and southern Colorado is rooted in colonial times, and hence it reflects archaisms linguistically connected to Spain. Evidence of this phenomenon is seen in words the old-timers habitually use, such as *naide* for *nadie* (nobody) and *cuasi* for *casi* (almost). But the Spanish spoken in this region has not remained static; its fluidity manifests in regionalisms that have been incorporated into our lexicon over many, many years. Words like *parquete/paquete* (package), *probe/pobre* (poor), and *murre/muy* (very) are common. Anglicisms are also prevalent: *cranque* for crank or *Crismes* for Christmas can be heard among Spanish-speakers of today. Mexicanisms (e.g., *dialtiro*) are not uncommon in New Mexico either.

Because a person reading a story in this dialect may wonder what the equivalent of a regional word is in the modern language, I have included a glossary that juxtaposes regional and so-called standard terms, which can be helpful even to the student of Spanish.

Regional Spanish	Standard Spanish	Regional Spanish	Standard Spanish
A case de	en casa de	alcol	alcohol
aá	allá	almiraban	admiraban
abusao	abusado	alredor	alrededor
acabalos	acabarlos	amá	mamá
aconsejalo	aconsejarlo	amanecites	amaneciste
agarrala	agarrarla	amarrale	amarrarle
aguantábanos	aguantábamos	andaa	andaba
aguantale	aguantarle	andáanos	andábamos
agüelita	abuelita	andábanos	andábamos
águila	astuto	andávanos	andábamos
ahi	ahí	animao	animado
ai	ahí	antonces	entonces
alberjón	guisante	apreviniendo	previniendo

Regional Spanish	Standard Spanish	Regional Spanish	Standard Spanish
apurao	apurado	colgao	colgado
arreglao	arreglado	Colorao	Colorado
arrentó	alquiló	comites	comiste
arriando	arreando	comprale	comprarle
arriva	arriba; encima	comprao	comprado
arrivita	un poco encima	comunidá	comunidad
asina	así	condao	condado
atarantao	atarantado	contoy	con todo y
atrás	detrás	contrataa	contratada
atroz	terrible	cortao	cortado
avisale	avisarle	creo	credo
ayudale(s)	ayudarle(s)	creyes	crees
		Crismes	Navidad
Bailábanos	bailábamos	croque	creo que
barbaridá	barbaridad	cuadraba	gustaba
basuderos	basureros	cuidao	cuidado
batallao	batallado	culeca	clueca
bato	muchacho	curre	corre
bendiciera	bendijera		
bendicilo	bendecirlo	D'ella	de ella
buscale	buscarle	d'ellos	de ellos
		d'eos	de ellos
Cabeciando	cabeceando	d'esa	de esa
'cabó	acabó	d'esos	de esos
cacaguate	cacahuate	d'este	de este
'char	echar	dale	darle
caiban	caían	de ende	de donde
cáisele	se le cayó	decile	decirle
cambiale	cambiarle	dejalo	dejarlo
caminao	caminado	demontres	diablos
cansaos	cansados	descoger	escoger
carriadores	acarreadores	diatiro	dialtiro
casao(s)	casado(s)	dicía	decía
catacismo	catecismo	dicilas	decirlas
chequiar	chequear	dicilos	decirlos
chequié	chequeé	dicir	decir
chicotiándole	chicotéandole	diciles	decirles
clas	clase	diferenciábanos	diferenciábamos

Regional Spanish	Standard Spanish	Regional Spanish	Standard Spanish
dijía(n)	decía(n)	envoltió	volteó
dijieron	dijeron	eos	ellos
dijir	decir	éranos	éramos
dijites	dijiste	esperencia	experiencia
dijunto	difunto	estaa	estaba
dionde	de donde	estáanos	estábamos
disierto	desierto	estábanos	estábamos
dites	diste	estafeta	correos
diún	de un	estao	estado
diuna vez	de una vez; pronto	Faceto	jactancioso
dotor	doctor	feria	cambio
duce	dulce	feriaban	cambiaban
durmía	dormía	fuites	fuiste
Eas	ellas	Garramos	ganar (dinero)
echábanos	echábamos	garró	agarró; ganó
echao	echado	gaselín	gasolina
edá	edad	golpiaba	golpeaba
empresté	presté	gotiaba	goteaba
en papá	papá	granpo	abuelito
en peloto	desnudo	güelta	vuelta
en redondo	alrededor de	güélvamelo	devuélvamelo
en wal de	en vez de	güelvo	vuelvo
enbocando	embocar	güen(o)	buen(o)
enbócate	embócate	güevón	huevón; flojo
enboco	emboco	güevos	huevos
enbocó	embocó		
enbolao	embolado; borracho	Ha	he
		ha de	he de
enbusteros	embusteros	hacela	hacerla
enjertar	injertar	hacele	hacerle
enpezaron	empezaron	haiga	haya
enpezó	empezó	hallao	hallado
enseñale	enseñarle	helao	helado
enterrala	enterrarla	hielera	refrigerador
entrao	entrado	'hijao	ahijado
entrates	entraste	hogando	ahogando

Regional Spanish	Standard Spanish	Regional Spanish	Standard Spanish
horita	ahorita	ladiao	ladeado
hundiaron	hundieron	ladié	ladeé
		lambidas	lamidas
Íbanos	íbamos	lao(s)	lado(s)
introdució	introdujo	lego	luego
intuertos	dolores de parto	lelo	leerlo
invitaos	invitados	libertá	libertad
isque	dizque	limitao	limitado
iva(n)	iba(n)	logo	luego
iyendo	yendo	loo	luego
		l'otra	la otra
Jalara	halara	l'otro	el otro
jallaba(n)	hallaba(n)	l'último	el último
jallamos	hallamos		
jallan	hallan	Llegao	llegado
jallao	hallado	llevaan	llevaban
jallar	hallar	llevala	llevarla
jallará	hallará		
jallaron	hallaron	Maiz	maíz
jallo	hallo	malcriao	malcriado
jalló	halló	maldá	maldad
jaló	haló	mamases	mamás
jediondo	hediondo	mana	hermana
jue	fue	mandao	mandado
'juera	afuera	manía	mañía
juera	afuera; fuera	mano	hermano
jueron	fueron	mascáranos	mascáramos
juertes	fuertes	matao	matado
jui	fui	matates	mataste
juimos	fuimos	medecina	medicina
juir	huir	meniale	menearle; pegarle
juites	fuiste	mestro	maestro
junte	junto	mi 'jito	mi hijito
juyendo	huyendo	mojao	mojado
juyéndole	huyéndole	muncho	mucho
		muremos	morimos
L'agua	el agua	murirse	morirse
l'ahogó	la ahogó	mure	muy

Regional Spanish	Standard Spanish	Regional Spanish	Standard Spanish
murre	muy	pasaos	pasados
		pasiando	paseando
Naa	nada	pasiándose	paseándose
naguas	enaguas	pasiar(se)	pasear(se)
naide	nadie	patrás	para atrás
niuno	ní uno	pedíorico	periódico
'nojada	enojada	pegale	pegarle
'nojao	enojado	pegao	pegado
'nojar	enojar	pelaa	pelada
nojó	enojó	peliaba	peleaba
nojotras(os)	nosotras(os)	peliaron	pelearon
nomás	solamente	pensates	pensaste
		pesao	pesado
Ocupao	ocupado	pescoliaban	pescaban; agarra-
oido	oído		ban
oílo	oirlo	pidía	pedía
olvidao	olvidado	pior	peor
onde	donde	pos	pues
oroplanos	aeroplanos	preguntale	preguntarle
oyelo	oirlo	probe	pobre
oyer	oir	prometeles	prometerles
		publicao	publacdo
Pa	para	puché	empujé
pa 'prendelo	para prenderlo	pudrío	podrido
paá	para allá	puercos	sucios
pacá	para acá	pus	pues
pacencia	paciencia	pusites	pusiste
pa'cer	para hacer		
pais	país	Quedrá(s)	querrá(s)
pal	para el	quitale	quitarle
pallá	para allá		
panteras	elegantes	Reciecito	muy recio
papases	papás	redepente	de repente
papel	periódico	reditió	derritió
par	para	reló	reloj
parao	parado	renegada	mal hablada
parquete	paquete	repartemos	repartimos
parva	montón	respondele	responderle

Regional Spanish	Standard Spanish	Regional Spanish	Standard Spanish
resurates	rasuraste	trabajavan	trabajaban
rezao	rezado	trai	trae
riyera	riera	traiba(n)	traía(n)
robao	robado	traque	ferrocarril
ronpele	romperle	trompezó	tropezó
		troquita	camioneta
Sacalos	sacarlos	truje	traje
salida	sin respeto	trujiera	trajera
saliles	salirles	trujo	trajo
sampé	zampé		
sanao	sanado	Un'orilla	una orilla
sembrao	sembrado	usaan	usaban
sentao	sentado	usté	usted
siguía	seguía		
silleta	silla	Vacales	muchas vacas
subemos	subimos	veiga	vea
suidá	ciudad	vejículo	vehículo
		velaan	velaban
'Taa	todavía	velo	verlo
'táanos	estábamos	verdá	verdad
'taba	estaba	vía	veía
tamién	también	vido	vio
tapada	estúpida	vinía(n)	venía(n)
tavía	todavía	vinido	venido
telefón	teléfono	vinir	venir
telefonió	telefoneó	vinites	viniste
tenelo	tenerlo	visitalo	visitarlo
teníanos	teníamos	vistir	vestir
tiórica	plática; charla	vivíanos	vivíamos
tirates	tiraste	voltiar	voltear
toa(s)	toda(s)	voltiara	volteara
toavía	toavía	voltié	volteé
tocalas	tocarlas	voltió	volteó
tomao	tomado; borracho		
too(s)	todo(s)	Zurró	cagó
trabajale	trabajarle		
trabajao	trabajado		